The Road to Lame Deer

For Brian Peterson —

with best wishes and encouragement

Terry Mader

04/15/03

The Road

to

Lame Deer

Jerry Mader

UNIVERSITY OF NEBRASKA PRESS

LINCOLN AND LONDON

Excerpt from "Little
Gidding" in Four Quartets,
copyright 1942 by T. S. Eliot
and renewed 1970 by Esme
Valerie Eliot, reprinted by
permission of Harcourt, Inc.,
and Faber and Faber Limited.

Photographs © Jerry Mader
unless otherwise specified.
Illustrations 37–44 are from
the Buffalo Bill Historical
Society, Cody WY, and origi-
nally appeared in Thomas B.
Marquis, The Cheyennes of
Montana (Algonac MI: Reference Publications, 1978), 81,
133, 144. Reprinted with
permission.

Library of Congress Cataloging-
in-Publication Data

Mader, Jerry, 1944–
The road to Lame Deer /
Jerry Mader.
p. cm.
Includes bibliographical references.
ISBN 0-8032-3103-7 (cloth: alk paper)
1. Cheyenne Indians. 2. Mader,
Jerry, 1944– 3. Cheyenne Indians—
Portraits. 4. Lame Deer (Mont.)
I. Title.
E99.C53 M33 2002
978.004′973—dc21   2002017983

In Memoriam
Henry Tall Bull
and
Tom Weist

Contents

Preface

To have written this book is to have kept at last a promise I first made some twenty-five years ago. Each year for a decade, with utter sincerity, I promised myself to write a book about my experiences with the Northern Cheyennes in Montana, a book that would complement the photographs I'd made of Cheyenne elders in the early 1970s. Obviously, it turned out to be a difficult promise to keep.

When I left Montana in 1977, over a year had passed since my last day on the reservation and more than five since I'd first traveled the road to Lame Deer. My Lame Deer experiences were still fresh in my mind, however, and the photographs already spoke for themselves. I was hopeful. I took my promise and the photographs with me to Seattle and really believed that geographic and psychological distance would afford the necessary perspective. But with each passing year I found those faces that had called me in the first place once again resisting all my efforts to find words eloquent enough to share their presence. Finally, ten years away from Montana and the Cheyennes, I stopped promising.

For ten more years the project lay dormant, with the negatives in storage and only one surviving print in view: a sixteen-by-twenty-inch print of Bessie Elkshoulder that hung in my studio as a permanent reminder of what I believed would elude me forever. I gave up. But the faces did not. They waited for me somewhere deep inside until I was ready for them and for the revelatory discovery— however obvious it seems now—that only the *act* of writing could release what I had repressed for so long.

In sum, writing meant that I would have to face the issues I could not face twenty years before, issues surrounding white Americans' past and present relationships with Native Americans, which are still rife with failure, heartbreak, and frustration for all parties concerned. Therefore, writing meant that I would finally have to go, as American Indian Movement founder Russell Means recently said in his autobiography, "where white men fear to tread." When at last I accepted that commitment, this book came furiously and without restraint.

Now, having completed the work, I see that the issues remain. When I began, I believed, at least a little, that the writing of this book might provide the answers I could not find when the events recorded here occurred, or at least a new way of confronting xenophobia head on. Sadly, no answers or miracles emerged from the process. What is evident, however, is that little has changed for Native Americans since the 1970s. Indeed, the white community's general silence regarding the continuing struggle of Native people on reservations in America confirms my general disappointment and exasperation in the face of humanity's resistance to change. Americans, it seems, cannot define themselves without making fateful and fatal distinctions between us and them.

I have learned, though, that however disappointed I may be, moral invective does little to promote change. Love of our neighbors, those who are not like us, will not precipitate from the injunction to love. Love is behavior, not pronouncement; as proof of that distinction we need only consider our response to the current squalor of our inner cities, the continuing blight that is the American Indian reservation, and, beyond these, the plight of the so-called third world. We care for others so long as they support our right to unimpeded self-interest—a right which, of course, we claim is available to anyone in any ghetto who is willing to work.

Not even the threat of losing certain cultures has mobilized us. Citing the phenomenon of cultural extinction among indigenous peoples worldwide as further evidence of the wave of extinction currently engulfing the natural world has generally failed to move anyone beyond the meaningful sigh or the thoughtful head-shake. Many Americans, particularly the ones driving the corporate, technological engine, believe that they can not only control nature but survive without it. They believe that no matter what the consequence of human dominance, their applied science will solve the mysteries of life. If all natural habitats are transformed and most species disappear, science will simply reshape the environment anew to even greater human advantage.

And so, whatever I might offer now in response to the issues I confronted in Lame Deer seems as impotent within the current general silence as it did in the 1970s. Few of my contemporaries are willing even to consider the plight of native cultures within the current process of "globalization." Despite our collective history or my despair, however, the Native nations survive and persist in their efforts to preserve their traditions. In the words of the Gros Ventre activist George Horse Capture, "We are here now, have been here for thousands of years, and we will always be here. We have fooled them all."

And so have the Northern Cheyennes. They are still in possession of their land, despite white encroachment and the temptation to sell their entitlement for temporary economic relief. In the thirty years since I first traveled the road to Lame Deer, their population there has remained stable, and the community has worked hard to improve its status. Lame Deer now has a fully accredited junior college, a community health center, a drug and alcohol treatment center, a new high school, a tribal capital complex, and a full-service bank.

Difficulties remain, however, despite anyone's optimism. In addition to persistent racial discrimination from the surrounding white community, alcoholism still gnaws away at the general health of the people. And now, with its coupling to methamphetamines and crack cocaine, the scourge of addiction has added force and long-term consequences. School attendance is still a problem, and younger Cheyennes who are fluent in their native language become fewer with each generation. Finally, it is common knowledge that the Northern Cheyenne reservation sits atop the largest deposit of low-sulfur bituminous coal in North America. With every passing year the pressure from Big Sky Coal, Peabody Coal, and Montana Power pushes younger Cheyennes closer to selling their land to the developers—a move that would effectively dissolve the reservation altogether.

My darkest moments, therefore, come when I realize how many young Cheyennes will lose their future and their lives as a consequence of addiction, and when I consider the persistent indifference or disdain of the white community. The difficulties I encountered in Lame Deer have not been relieved by this writing but, rather, sharpened by the process. As William Faulkner said, "His-

tory is not a *was*, history *is*." Neither I nor you nor we can escape the
history embedded in what I have remembered here, because it is
with us now. It cannot be relegated to the past as an irrelevant *was*,
because it reveals a xenophobic American psyche that must be
transformed if the good life is to be available for all. Redefining
who and what we are could make all the difference.

As a plausible item for this wide agenda, therefore, I offer
The Road to Lame Deer. I offer it primarily out of respect for the
Cheyenne people and their elders who are pictured here. I also
offer it, with gratitude, *to* them. My life has been richly informed
and profoundly transformed by the grace of their generosity, humor, spirit, and courage. This is a debt not easily repaid. But it is
my hope that these photographs and what I have remembered and
considered in this writing will at least reflect the magnitude of that
debt and therefore aid, somehow, the Cheyenne people as they
continue to sustain their autonomy.

What I have said about them is the product of my experience,
not theirs; what it truly means to be Cheyenne must be given over
to their voices. Therefore, I hope that this offering will not only
spur genuine response from the white community but encourage
Cheyennes to tell their stories as well. Humanity's struggle for the
good life on Planet Earth will be impoverished in unspeakable ways
if the world view resonant in their voices is not heard.

Most of those pictured here are dead, and as I view them all now,
the poet Paul Bowles's voice rings true: "Everything happens only
a certain number of times, and a very small number, really. How
many times will you remember a certain afternoon of your childhood, some afternoon that's so deeply a part of your being that
you can't even conceive of your life without it? Perhaps four or
five times more. Perhaps not even that. How many more times
will you watch the full moon rise? Perhaps twenty. And yet it all
seems limitless." Looking at these photographs reminds me that
all the people I've loved who are now gone died in my absence.
Time is our enemy in all this because not only do we not know how
many of that "very small number" remain available but we cannot know which is indeed the last time, the last moonrise, the last
conversation.

I have been fortunate because of those I've loved who are now
gone, each one has expanded rather than diminished my existence. Each had much to teach me and gave that knowledge gen-

erously. And the absence of each brings me a different kind of loss and grief. In the wake of their passing I measure my own steps differently.

Here, then, is my story, and here are the faces that contain the living stories of their people. They call themselves Tse-tsėhésė-staestse: the people like us or, simply, like us. May they be heard.

Acknowledgments

I think I can safely say that this book has demanded more of me than any other project I've attempted in my career. As a personal odyssey and emotional catharsis it has been quite a ride. For that reason, there are people who deserve mention here because they have patiently seen me through the cycles of mania and depression that permeated the writing.

First, thanks to those stalwart members of my family who kept their distance or moved in close as it seemed necessary to them: Stacie Lorenson, Charles Norton, Laura Roe, and Lar Mader. From my sullen, reclusive point of view their responses were impeccable. Second, thanks to three friends who cheered from a distance: David Morse, John Grinder, and Jean Belangie-Nye. Third, thanks to Michael Colgrass, who knew I was a writer long before I did. And, of course, my thanks to the folks at the University of Nebraska Press who at last helped bring this project to completion.

Next, it is certain that there would be no book without the photographs, and no photographs without the indomitable influence of the late Lee Nye. It was he who brought the reality of photography as a vital art form home to me, and it was he who persistently harangued me from his lair in Missoula, Montana, no matter where I tried to hide. As my teacher, friend, and colleague he was one of those precious few stewards of the human spirit who kept it well. His uncompromising passion for art and life were transformative influences. His friendship was without parallel and my privilege to enjoy for thirty years. I regret that he did not live to see this project completed. I miss him more than I can say.

This book would not exist at all, however, without Tom Weist, who provided my crucial first introduction to the Northern Cheyennes and reservation life. He was my traveling companion on the road to Lame Deer, and our friendship was forged through each of those journeys. His understanding of Cheyenne history and culture was an invaluable source of practical wisdom as I found my way through the intricacies of another society. Sadly, he died before this book was written.

Tom and I had talked many times of collaborating on a book about our Lame Deer experiences, and so I have an odd sense of déjà vu now that the project is complete. Apart from serving as a record of our time together, I hope it will also remind the Northern Cheyennes and anthropological community in Montana of Tom's extensive service and contributions to the tribe and to western history. His *History of the Cheyenne People* is still in use in Lame Deer schools and Dull Knife Memorial College; his work with Henry Tall Bull, which produced several books of Cheyenne children's stories, was an invaluable cultural contribution; and his edition of Thomas B. Marquis's previously unpublished *The Cheyennes of Montana* is a fine addition to Native studies. Morever, it was because of his interest that the Marquis collection of photographs was preserved, and my participation in their restoration is an experience I shall never forget.

I must also extend my thanks to Tom's first wife, Katherine (Tobie) M. Weist, professor emeritus of anthropology at the University of Montana–Missoula. Her doctoral fieldwork on the Northern Cheyenne reservation precipitated Tom's continued involvement with the tribe, which in turn brought Tom into my life. But more than that, she offered sound perspective and friendship to me as I learned about the Cheyennes.

Of course, the Cheyenne people themselves deserve more than my thanks can express, for it was they who opened their homes and their hearts to me, particularly Henry and Irene Tall Bull, John Woodenlegs, Richard Littlebear, and all the elders who allowed me to make photographs of them. Thanks also to Tim Cook of Busby, Montana, whose comprehensive work on Cheyenne genealogy was invaluable. And special thanks to Richard Littlebear and Bill Wertman for their assistance in establishing, at Dull Knife Memorial College in Lame Deer, an educational fund in the names of Henry Tall Bull and Tom Weist. I plan to allocate a portion of the proceeds from sales of this book and of the photographs to that fund.

Finally, my abiding gratitude to my wife, Stephanie, who knows every craven recess of my being and loves me anyway.

The Road to Lame Deer

PART I
Of Absence and Return

1

> And the end of all our exploring
> Will be to arrive where we started
> And know the place for the first time.
>
> T. S. ELIOT

I knew it was the last time. I knew it the way you know, long before it is declared, that a love affair is over; or the way you know, long after the burial, that the one you have loved is completely and utterly dead. That kind of knowledge makes you do queer things — things you do so you won't have to face the facts of death and failure.

And so, within that certain knowledge, I protracted my last journey to Lame Deer. I dawdled all the way from Missoula, pausing along the road at odd places, unconsciously avoiding the memorable ones where I'd stopped the car and rushed into the landscape to capture an image on film before the particular motivating light shifted and inspiration became yet another scenic postcard.

It was the first trip to Lame Deer I'd made in the complete absence of Tom Weist or Henry Tall Bull; one or the other had always been in the front seat with me or waiting at the other end. I dawdled through each of the 450 miles like a child on his way home from school to an empty house.

I didn't want to hear the story. I didn't want to hear it as much as I knew I had to listen. And I recognized, as I drove across Lame Deer Creek that morning, that this kind of necessity had generally characterized every journey I'd made to the reservation, a necessity whose unique imperatives were somehow heightened each time I entered the world of the Cheyennes. This time the story and its truth were already known, and facing that truth was going to be more painful than just knowing it. I knew that facing all the stories was, in the end, why I had journeyed in the first place. But that morning was different. I was by then a part of those stories. Henry Tall Bull was one I'd loved, and he was dead, and I had to listen to his wife, Irene, tell the story of his dying. And although I knew it wasn't true, I felt that somehow I had failed him.

I drove slowly past the Lame Deer Cafe and the IGA and thought about the traditional Cheyenne response to death. Since the time before the reservation, their answer has been the same: death is but one more confirmation of the unity of spirit in all things. And their belief continues in spite of Christian influence. For the Cheyennes, death reaffirms kinship within the people. Any death is an influence upon all relationships; no death is limited to a single family. No one dies alone.

The old ways said that when death comes, the lodge of the bereaved and its contents must be abandoned. Only personal items that would be interred with the deceased were to be kept; everything else was given away. The home might remain empty for months, sometimes for a year, before the family returned; often they never did.

When a child or a spouse died, members of the immediate family (usually the surviving spouse or the parents) slashed their forearms, legs, and faces or sometimes cut off the tip of a finger. Widows often cut their hair short. Then followed, after the burial and "giveaway," a period of wandering from lodge to lodge, where tribal kin fed and generally assisted those in mourning. At every stop the bereaved told the story of their loved one's death and confirmed again and again their homelessness and grief.

The wandering often continued for many weeks or months, sometimes as long as a year, before the family settled into a new home. Then relatives and friends came, bringing all the necessary articles and provisions for homemaking as the newly configured family was reabsorbed into the tribe.

The experience of the deceased was believed to be parallel to that of the bereaved. Like the mourners finding their way back into the community of the living, the spirit of the dead one needed to find its way into the world of all spirits—an indeterminate journey requiring frequent rest and sustenance. The grave, therefore, had to be above ground, the body wrapped in blankets or skins and covered with stones placed so the spirit might enter and exit with ease. Favorite articles from life were placed around the body: clothing, tools, sacred objects, tobacco, and food. The spirit within the food and tobacco would feed and calm the spirit of the deceased as it made its way to its place in the spirit world. Without this nourishment and occasional rest within the grave, the spirit risked exhaustion and its own death—a finality too dark for contemplation.

From the beginning of the reservation period, self-wounding and open-air interment were systematically suppressed by missionaries and Bureau of Indian Affairs (BIA) officials. But, as with all white influences, the Cheyennes yielded without essentially rejecting the old ways. Few now wound themselves, and white-style cemeteries have replaced open stone graves, but the essentials of traditional mourning remain: the giveaway, occasional relocation, and storytelling from house to house.

In front of Henry's house that morning, I sat inside the car for a long time. Curtains covered all the windows. Wind spun the ubiquitous red Lame Deer dust across the empty yard. The small front porch still sported three tattered dinette chairs and the rough oak table that had supported countless deer carcasses while Henry artfully butchered them and pitched scraps to the crowd of reservation dogs that belonged to everyone and no one, who lived everywhere and nowhere. Henry's house looked closed, but I knew Irene was waiting.

The neighborhood, always quiet, seemed overtly hushed and somehow expectant. The houses were in the typically unplatted arrangement of most Cheyenne neighborhoods, reflecting clusters of kinship rather than urban geometry. Everyone knows who is at home at any given time, even though no one seems to be watching. And so I knew that behind the closed doors and drawn window shades, inside their quiet homes, inside the singular stillness of that day, they all knew I was there.

Henry had taught me the Cheyenne way of visitation, and his pedagogy was also in the old way—by example and stories, never through injunctions or explanations. He admonished me only once. We had spent an hour in conversation with some older Cheyenne men on the steps of the Lame Deer Cafe, and I had offered a cigarette to just one of the men before lighting up myself. "If you don't offer to all, they will think you're stingy!"

I waited in the car and gave Irene time. I too needed to prepare for the story she was going to tell. I had brought a gift—the portrait I'd made of Henry, which he'd enjoyed showing to visitors, each time announcing, "Look, Charles Bronson!" As I stepped out of the car, a red dust devil spun through the front yard and collapsed at the edge of the road.

Henry's car was still parked where I'd left it over three years before and had achieved permanent status as part of the landscape. Almost two years had passed since I'd visited Lame Deer, and now all the hesitation that had colored my return was attacking my legs. I leaned on my car, fumbled for a cigarette, started to light it, then put it away. I looked at the hill behind me and tried to remember how many afternoons we had spent sitting on the porch watching the colors change on that hill. And with that, I felt another reluctance. I didn't want to remember everything, but I knew that whatever she said, each of her words would release the memories, and I would have to face them all again. At last, I gave up and walked to the porch. My hand rose and completed one knock just as the door moved under it.

Irene's oval face looked up and around in the small opening and regarded me as one expected but sorely overdue for a visit.

"Oooh Jerry—come in, come in!"

I entered and stood awkwardly in the half-light. My eyes struggled to find her as she brought a dinette chair for me and then moved through the room with short arthritic steps to her place in the center. We sat opposite, and I kept my eyes from her as she took a set of photos from her purse.

As she prepared to speak, the shaded windows and walls seemed slowly to fall away, leaving Irene and me alone at the center of Henry's obituary. She sat straight. Her black eyes, fierce against the tears, looked directly into the void around us. Her arthritic forearms and hands seemed more twisted than ever, her deformed fingers oddly placid atop the stack of Polaroid photos in her lap.

As her soft measured tones marked each detail of the story, she handed a picture to me. Each snapshot presented a different point of view; all of them displayed Henry in his coffin. Her meticulous narrative progressed; my hands filled with photographs; and I slowly lost the continuity of it all, her voice finally a gentle buzzing at the periphery of the circle of shade around us. At last I choked on my own breath, startled by my sudden awareness of amnesia and the silence.

We had been silent for a long time. Irene, with her eyes still fixed somewhere beyond Lame Deer, was rocking slowly and humming a peyote song just above the horizon of audibility.

I was embarrassed and ashamed. I had disappeared under the monologue and retreated into some insulated internal place where the story couldn't reach me. When consciousness returned, I struggled for words within my cowardice. I was appalled by the poverty of responses available to me. What I was able to say seemed worse than platitude, but I was unwilling to offer the typical clichés celebrating the grieving process and eternal life. Those responses, typically so repressive, hide a deeper unwillingness to come to terms with death at all; we speak as if, through artful deletion, the specter will finally just go away, so we can all go on pretending that death isn't real.

Irene was secure in the Cheyenne way. And so she could tell the story, and tell it again, until his spirit found its way and hers found comfort after there was no more telling to be done.

Henry had died in the ambulance on the way from the Forsyth jail to the hospital—or so it was said. The reports were confused. Some said he had lain unconscious in jail for three days before the police called the ambulance. Others said he'd been badly and expertly beaten, the way certain thugs and some policemen know how to beat a man so that there are few external signs but massive internal damage. The police said he'd fallen into an alcoholic coma after he was arrested for fighting in the street. There was no autopsy. There was no inquest.

When I handed the Polaroids back to Irene, I realized that in all our time together I had not managed to make a photograph of her. And I knew that that possibility, along with many others not realized, would be committed to oblivion that morning. She managed a smile when I gave her Henry's portrait. "I'm going to live in Ashland with my sister. My arthritis is getting bad. He said the only time he had fun was when you and Tom came down."

The first time, we had driven from Missoula along the ragged edges of January, and Tom filled each mile with a virtually seamless monologue that blended Cheyenne history, his wife's anthropological fieldwork on the reservation, his work with Henry Tall Bull on the writing project, all manner of photographic possibilities for me, and his reiterated willingness to stop the car at any time should I see something worthy of a picture. And as each new subject was launched, he paused and insisted, "I usually don't talk this much."

But he couldn't stop himself. Tom's enthusiasm for Cheyenne culture was unrestrained, and so he went on for at least two hours, apprising me of his involvement with cultural activities on the reservation.

After Tobie's fieldwork was completed, Tom's parallel interests had earned him several invitations to help the tribe with educational projects. The newly formed Northern Cheyenne Research and Human Development Association had received a grant from the Johnson-O'Malley Foundation to collect stories and songs. These would be preserved as audio recordings and then put into book form. Also, under the 1964 Equal Opportunity Act, many educational projects had been started, including a bilingual program in the Busby school district. Tom's understanding of Cheyenne history and his writing skill made him an attractive choice as adviser and writer for many of these programs. He was currently involved in the production of booklets of traditional children's stories and a much-needed history of the Cheyenne people for use in the schools.

After Tobie accepted a position at the University of Montana, Tom began commuting once a month from Missoula to Lame Deer for cultural association or writing project meetings. The 450-mile drive can be daunting, and he was grateful for my company.

His talk was welcome. We didn't know each other very well yet, and in truth I had few purposes beyond my own curiosity and hope for fresh photographic subjects. At least that's what I told myself. And yet, as we pressed on toward the center of the state, an unspecified uneasiness began to fester in me. I was suddenly aware of the wider implications of what I was doing, and the midwinter sky only seemed to sharpen the contradictions implicit within Indian and white history in Montana. Those contradictions loomed larger as we got closer to our destination and I realized how little I had considered my intentions for this journey.

By the time we reached Livingston, halfway to Lame Deer, my uncertainties about where or for what purpose this road would or should take me were breeding claustrophobia in my guts. I could feel it rising toward my throat as the car windows began to crowd in around me.

I asked Tom to stop the car. I didn't tell him what I really wanted, which was to turn around and go home. Instead, I pointed to the mountains and reached for my camera. He found a wide spot, and I jumped out just ahead of my panic. I walked a few paces from the car and pretended to frame a photograph.

The sky was shifting toward whiteout. A blizzard was coming. The mountain wall was shrouded in veils of cloud still transparent enough to make ghosts of the peaks. In the lull before a blizzard on the high plains, the approaching storm pushes warm air out in front of itself—a springtime too brief to fool anyone. I let it blow over me and hoped it would ease my inner turmoil.

It failed. At the eye of the storm within, I found little beyond ignorance and a determination to photograph people as they were, unguarded, without pretense. That's what I told myself. But as I stared into the vastness around me, it was obvious I had no idea what I was doing. The distance between anything and everything else in Montana, including its inhabitants, achieved metaphorical precision as I confronted my ignorance. There were seven Indian reservations in the state, and I had seen none of them. I had no reference experiences to call upon, just the vague sense of repressed guilt most white Montanans share as the consequence of our painful history with Indians.

And so, as the first gust of the storm bit my cheek, I found the source of my angst. As a white man with a camera, who could be so easily perceived as just another white man once again invading, once again wanting to take something, I had a lot of context to build if I were to learn anything at all, let alone make photographs.

By the time I returned to the car, the Crazy Mountains to the north had disappeared inside the whiteout. We still had over two hundred miles to go, and the storm was going to chase us. We didn't slow down except for a quick fuel stop in Billings. And then, as the road climbed out of the Yellowstone valley, skirted the edge of the rimrocks above the city, and turned to the southeast, the storm threat relaxed, the sky opened, and I was awakened to a landscape I'd only read about.

This place had been the preferred hunting ground for Sioux, Crow, and Cheyenne. When Lewis and Clark approached the upper reaches of the Missouri River in 1803, this place was marked "Terra Incognita" on their maps. Seventy-five years later this was the place where the Sioux and Cheyennes lost their freedom on the great plains. As we headed away from Billings toward Hardin and the town of Crow Agency, the power of that landscape captured me, and it was easy to understand why the Plains tribes had wanted to live here forever. It was as if we drove perpetually at the edge of the world, balancing, delicately poised atop the line dividing earth and sky.

The sun was low when we at last turned off I-90 onto U.S. 212 at Crow Agency. Tom drove slowly as we passed the Custer Battlefield. I tried to see the white stone markers on the hillsides, but they were buried in snow. Tom, of course, had his own commentary about the place.

"Many of the Cheyennes who eventually reported the fight said Custer's soldiers panicked and shot themselves. Whoever actually killed Custer is still unknown, although White Bull, Sitting Bull's nephew, claimed he did it. Nonetheless, as the eyewitness reports came in over the decades, the so-called last stand turned out to be more propaganda than fact. Two Moon, a Cheyenne chief, said the whole thing lasted about as long as it takes a hungry man to eat his dinner."

Tom punched the accelerator as the battlefield disappeared from view. The snow clouds turned pink and blue behind us. "Well," he said, "you're on the road to Lame Deer now."

Even in winter, sunset takes a long time on the high plains. The hard crust of snow on the ground turned blue-white in the twilight as we crossed Rosebud Creek and then slowed down in front of the Busby General Store. About a mile north of the town, Custer had made his last camp before he marched to the Little Big Horn. Tom stopped the car and pointed to the shadowy brick buildings down the hill.

"That's the Busby school. It started as the first Agency boarding school just after the reservation was formed. Cheyenne kids were removed from their homes and housed at the school. As with other Indian assimilation programs, they weren't allowed to speak Cheyenne, their hair was cut, and they had to wear white man's clothes. Of course, all traditional ways were banned. The parents couldn't stand the separation, so they camped outside the school grounds in the early days. I guess that's how Busby became a town."

A few lights went on in the largest of the buildings as we eased back onto the highway. "Sixteen miles to go!" he said. I watched the twilight bounce off the frozen surface of Rosebud Creek as it briefly followed us and then turned to chase the sunset across the plains while the mountains went dark in the distance.

About three miles out of Lame Deer the road turns sharply and drops about two hundred feet into the basin of Lame Deer Creek.

As we made the turn, the headlights caught the first gusts of snow and then, at the bottom, as we turned toward the bridge, they illuminated the chain-link fence surrounding the BIA offices and government housing. The tribal police station and jail loomed through the light, and beyond them, yellow rectangles, the windows in the 1950s-style ranch-ramblers floated above the pale snow. At the bridge front the sign on the gate flashed as we turned: "Property of the United States Government Bureau of Indian Affairs. No Trespassing. Violators Will Be Prosecuted."

We crossed the creek and glided to a stop in front of the Lame Deer Cafe. The blizzard had caught us. I watched the street fill with snow while Tom talked about Chief Lame Deer.

"He was a Minneconjous Sioux and he came to the Big Horn River country when he heard there might be trouble with the soldiers. He wanted to be near Sitting Bull if there was going to be a big fight. That was in the spring of 1876. He didn't fight at the Little Big Horn, but after the battle he had to run from the soldiers like all the rest. A year later, General Miles caught up with him over there, where the Agency buildings are. The soldiers killed Lame Deer and a few of his warriors there. It's kind of funny. He came to help Sitting Bull, and then neither of them wound up fighting Custer."

Tom and I sat quietly in the car and watched the snow fall. Usually undaunted by the weather, as most Montanans say they are, we were suddenly wary under the silent white fury of the night sky.

Near the cafe was a house rented by two Upward Bound social workers. Tom had been staying with them on his monthly visits. We entered and found them hurriedly packing their bags for a hiatus in Billings, hoping to get off the reservation before the storm trapped them. They said they'd leave the door unlocked for us as they passed through it themselves.

Out in the street once more, Tom and I peered through the snow feathers at the approaching figure of Henry Tall Bull as it half-floated, half-stumbled over the deep snow ruts in the street. The earflaps on his fur-lined cap stood out straight from the sides of his head, and his arms, bound by the bulk of his down-filled coat, bounced away from his sides like those of a child who has been overdressed for winter by his mother.

The flakes were getting smaller as he called to us: "Come to the house—Irene has supper ready!"

It was a feast. Indeed, after nine hours of truck stop coffee and entrées à la grease, the mixture of traditional fry bread, vegetables, and southern fried chicken was a transcendent experience. And, I soon learned, my natural tendency to gluttony was received not only as high praise for Irene's cooking but as affirmation of Cheyenne generosity as well. I had won her heart with my appetite.

Tom, Henry, and Irene kept conversation moving through the dinner. I covered my uneasiness by keeping my mouth stuffed or by praising the cook when it wasn't. But eventually the talk came around to me and so, in lieu of explanations, I showed them the recent portrait I'd made of Belle Highwalking. It marked, after all, where my journey to Lame Deer had really begun, and so I had a story to tell.

I first saw Belle Highwalking on an early September Missoula afternoon on McLeod Avenue as she sat on Tom's front porch, directly across the street from my own. It was a few days before Labor Day, but the first frost had already arrived to snap the maples lining the street into their annual red-gold extravaganza. That afternoon swarmed with sweaty, grubby children trying to force a summer's worth of play into those last few hours before school started. The menagerie ran freely through my house with rug-rats of all dimensions pausing casually at the edge of my bathtub to view and critique my latest batch of prints as they spun through their final wash.

Among the spectators that day were two girls, Belle's granddaughters. When one asked about the pictures, I maneuvered my response into a request that she ask her grandmother if I could make a photograph of her. The girl said she would ask and then vanished into the maple leaves with the others. When she did not return and Belle disappeared into the house, I tried to plot alternatives.

By evening, it was an imperative. The camera had made me a hunter perpetually alert for that unspecified yet known change in light that transforms the ordinary into the unique, a hunter always searching for the faces, the ones through which the "glimpse" is possible—that quick look into eternal mortality. When I saw it jump at me across the thirty yards between my front porch and Tom's, the hunt was on. There would be no rest until the portrait was made.

But it was Tom who appeared in my basement studio that night full of questions, clearly protective of Belle. She had become very close with Tom's wife during the time of Tobie's fieldwork on the reservation. When that work was finished, Belle could not bear the separation and began a series of extended visits to Missoula. Then in her mid-seventies, Belle had spent her entire life on the reservation and most of that without ever speaking to a white person, so each trip was a challenging and somewhat frightful prospect. But her love for Tobie drove her on, and she always stayed as long as her supply of Lame Deer water lasted. Nonetheless, Belle remained wary of white people, particularly white men; their aggressive manner and loud talk frightened her.

By the end of the evening I had been duly warned but encouraged: Tom would speak with Belle and let me know. I offered to give prints to her family. Tom warned me about the long-term implications of that gesture and hoped I had a lot of paper.

A few days later, after all the children had gone to school, I stood before her on Tom's front porch with a camera in my hand, more uncertain about what I was doing than I had ever been. Belle looked at me just once, nodded quickly, then returned her eyes to her work.

The soft, pale buckskin was draped over her knees as her weathered fingers moved needle through beads and then, with one or several skewered, found the invisible line of the Morning Star pattern and pulled the thread until the click of glass announced their fixed position on it. Each movement was a deep, unconscious response to thoughts older than she, and as she lost herself in that ancient way, I found some ease, for not even the snap of the shutter could intrude upon the peace her mind secured along the taut thread and the parade of glass beads. At one point she held the needle and thread straight up from the hide, and her eyes looked out into the autumnal light filtering through the maple leaves on the avenue. She paused there for a very long moment and then found her way back to the next stitch, and the next and the next.

The buckskin vest would take over a year to complete, since every surface was to be covered with beaded design. A white man had commissioned the work, and Belle was impressed by the three-hundred-dollar fee he'd offered. She was delighted she could still earn money to help her grandchildren.

A few days later, as she was preparing to return to Lame Deer, I gave her a set of prints. She looked quickly, giggled behind the palm of her hand, and slid them back into the envelope. Then, with sudden courtesy, she nodded and said "thank you" and looked down at the envelope on her lap.

There was an odd silence after I stopped talking. Henry and Irene were completely absorbed in the portrait, unaware of Tom and me. At last, Tom suggested I might make portraits of some of the more important elders as a photographic project for the cultural association. Henry nodded, and then I received my first lesson in the direction of indirect communication, Cheyenne style:

"She looks so real . . . that's a good picture . . . my uncle would love to have that picture . . . Belle has a lot of grandchildren . . . that white man should pay more for the vest."

Suddenly, Tom and Henry realized they were late for their meeting, scheduled for 7:00 P.M. Henry noted that if they left right away they'd be only a few minutes late. It was 8:15. Tom reminded him that the meetings really never got going till 9:00. Irene laughed from the kitchen: "You're on Indian time now, Jerry!"

Tom grinned and went to the kitchen for another cup of coffee. Irene kept looking at the picture, marveling at how real Belle's hair looked. Henry went to the bedroom in search of his coat. I sat within the silent recognition that they were going to leave me alone with Irene. When they were finally suited up and ready to go, Tom saw my discomfort and smiled again. "These meetings tend to go on and on." Henry laughed and said, "Everybody has a story."

As they left, the snow pushed hard into the warm room and made a small triangular drift on the floor while the door closed. I watched it melt and remembered a piece of Tom's I-90 monologue:

> When the Cheyennes first saw white people on the plains, they called them the "Coodam People" because they heard them shouting "Coodam!" repeatedly as they drove their teams of oxen before them. Later, they learned that the white men were cursing their beasts and so they had to reconsider. There are no linguistic equivalencies in Cheyenne for English curse words. Over time, as they watched the settlers' wagon trains swarm across the plains like insects, they settled on calling them Vé'ho'e—Spider People—because the white man's clothing made him look all wrapped up, like a spider's cocoon.

I was alone with Irene Tall Bull, a strange white man alone with a Cheyenne woman. I didn't know if I was a Vé'ho'e, but I felt conspicuously known and named. She was right. I was on Indian time. Rather, I was in it for the first time, and the silence seemed endless as she sat near the dining room table, more still than any human I'd ever witnessed.

I sat at the end of the couch. She, slightly behind me, was just out of my vision. I was unsure. I felt the urge to be socially gracious, to make small talk, but was daunted by her silence. Somehow I knew she wasn't looking at me. My sense of time grew more and more acute. I wondered if I was being rude by not speaking. After several more minutes I adjusted my posture until she appeared in my peripheral vision.

Impossibly, she seemed even less mobile than before. Her hands rested on her lap, palms up, one on top of the other. Her small oval face was calm, her broad lips pursed slightly as if about to whistle or hum. Her eyes were fixed on some distant point beyond the closed door. She seemed completely at peace.

I returned to my original position and let the silence seep into me. I wondered how some of my "Type A" personality friends at the university would handle this silence. And I wondered if Irene's comfort within it was inherited from an older world where time was measured in seasons, by daylight and moonscape, within visitation, migration, play, the hunt, ceremony, and wind.

We continued in silence. I listened to the sounds of the house. A relatively new pre-fab tract house, designed for southern California, it was deeply engaged in its struggle with the wind. The temperature outside had reached the midteens, and so the gas heater was forced into nearly continuous production, pausing only occasionally for a few seconds as if catching its breath while the frigid fingers of the storm found every crack and open seam in the walls and window casings.

Henry and Irene had lived long portions of their adult lives off the reservation, but both had come of age just before World War II, the time their parents and grandparents called "the good old days." Although poverty was excessive then, alcoholism was rare, and their isolation allowed them to be nurtured in the old ways.

After the war many Cheyennes left the reservation in search of work, but kinship and familism inevitably drew them back; isolation inside white society was, in the end, more oppressive than poverty at home. It seemed so, at least, until poverty once again drove them off the reservation in search of opportunity. Henry and Irene had fallen into that cycle of absence and return to Lame Deer.

The house reflected their stance. Henry and Irene had used their claims money to acquire it and appoint it with "modern" conveniences. They prided themselves on their understanding of white society, their ease with white people, and took pleasure in enlightening their naive friends and elders still mystified by the Vé'ho'e. And so it was Irene's ability to live in two worlds that finally put me at ease that night.

Little by little I stopped searching for appropriate social graces. When simple physical exhaustion forced me to let go of the effort, Irene's complete comfort within that silence became obvious. Conversation was not required. She had made me feel welcome and at ease with her alone, and she had done it without speaking a word. As I would eventually learn, silence is ultimately respectful—for within it, listening is possible.

As my body steadily continued to match the stillness of hers, the comfort of good food and the warmth after winter chill pushed me into sleep. At least I thought I had dozed off when suddenly I was aware of Alex Black Horse seated next to Irene with little snow puddles circling his wet shoes. I was facing the front door but hadn't seen him come in, nor did it seem that Irene had moved. She introduced him to me, and we struggled for a few minutes with our mutual language barrier but managed cordial greetings. At last Irene came to the rescue and started a conversation with him in Cheyenne. I was quickly absorbed into the rhythm and music of the language.

They sat at a 45-degree angle, their eyes still, and looked not at each other but out into the space before them where their words floated above the stillness like wind over dry grass. The silence was now punctuated by waves of inflected speech, the listener in every exchange filling the pauses and marking the sequences with a singular syllable of support. The volume was a sustained mezzo-piano containing finely graded shades of tonal distinction, well above a whisper yet mindful of disturbance. It was the gentle talk we all seem to find beneath the sudden hush of twilight or at dawn, and inside it all I was seized again by what I'd seen at a distance in Missoula, emanating from Tom's front porch.

This time it came from Alex Black Horse's eyes—that ineffable glimpse. I looked at my camera bag on the floor next to the couch where I'd put it when we arrived. It might as well have been in Missoula. The complete lack of pretense in the man before me would admit nothing less than a gesture of respect that I did not know how to make. I had never seen such gentleness in a man before, and at that moment I relegated all plans for portraits to the dustbin.

When he disappeared as suddenly and magically as he had come, Irene smiled. "Alex is my uncle. He must be past seventy now." And then she giggled. "He's gonna tell everybody I had a white man in my house while Henry was gone!" She giggled again, betraying her delight at the prospects for gossip and sexual innuendo. "Let them talk all they want! I'll just let them wonder!"

The stillness enveloped us again, and she giggled once more just before the sudden knock at the door and muffled calling of her name brought her to her feet. I got my first view then of the damage her arthritis had done as she forced her body to the door. She opened it a crack and peeked around the edge and then eased back into the room as a man came in. She obviously knew him well but did not appear glad to see him.

He was young, in his early twenties, and wore a battered straw cowboy hat and a windbreaker much too light for the weather. He greeted me. I offered a cigarette; he refused. His manner was urgent but apologetic as he began to speak. He managed to get two or three halting phrases out in Cheyenne. He wanted something, but from the look on his face when she cut him off, he never got a chance to ask.

The ensuing firestorm of verbiage shattered my idyllic trance and silenced the wind. As a demonstration of the righteous indignation and humiliation that can happen when the real truth goes public, Irene Tall Bull's harangue was without parallel, and it needed no translation. The power of the Cheyenne matriarchy was irrefutable. He did not answer back but stood there in another kind of trance and weathered the onslaught. Although he held himself quite still and did not look at her or me, I saw her words sting at the corners of his eyes. When she paused, he said something nearly inaudible and moved toward the door, where he halted briefly to receive a final salvo of invective.

After the door had closed behind him, Irene made no apologies. "He's my nephew. He should take care of his grandmother but he wants money so he can go to Billings and go on a bender!" She turned stiffly, went into the kitchen, and made coffee. The silence returned.

I was grateful. This was a woman whose wrath I hoped I would never feel. And this was a woman whose favor I suddenly wanted more than I could comprehend. I was doubly grateful when a cup of coffee magically appeared on the end table next to me. And then I felt the deep comfort in her voice as it drifted lightly above the low moan of the wind.

She was in the kitchen behind me, humming to herself, finishing the dishes. The wind stopped and then started again. She asked if I had children. I looked at the picture on the small table in the corner while she told me about her daughter and granddaughter, how bright the baby was, how her daughter was going to beauty school in Billings. In the color photograph they looked like every other mother and baby posed to display the same baby giggle, the same maternal smile. Irene hummed some more, and I watched the drapery in front of the window billow as the draft slid along the wall. The heater shut off when the wind died again, and I counted the seconds while the icy draft raced along the floor and down the hall to the thermostat. It clicked, and the heater groaned and cycled again. "Boy . . . it's getting cold outside . . . I hope Alex got home all right." I tried to respond as he had, with just a soft round sound, and then Irene asked if I had pictures of my children. I heard her shuffle toward the living room while I fumbled for my wallet. She cooed over the pictures and told me how beautiful my daughter was and how handsome was my son. And then she sat in the dinette chair again beside the couch, and we both stared at the wall in front of us, and she hummed again and said, "You should bring your family down to visit sometime. Henry loves kids—he used to be scoutmaster. Your family could stay with us, we have lots of room. Maybe you could go to a pow-wow." I smiled, and she started humming again. I stared at the faded paint that failed to cover the signs of decay at the edge of the window frame. I looked at the hole in the door near the bottom; it looked as if it had been kicked in. The wind shifted a bit, and a thin wisp of fine snow slid through the threshold. I remembered long winter Sunday afternoons when I was a child when my father stood silently in the kitchen and looked out one window at nothing at all, while my mother sat at the dining room table and looked out that window at nothing at all, while snow fell and hours passed with less than a dozen words between them, and I was safe inside their unspoken knowledge of each other.

And then the door opened, and the wind pushed Tom and Henry into the room while they laughed about the tangential disorder so typical of the meetings. They left their coats on until the fresh coffee warmed them. The talk turned steadily toward the weather. The Upward Bound workers had been right: the storm was no longer just a threat. If we stayed, we'd spend the rest of January in Lame Deer. We said our goodbyes and made a run for it.

The snow blew hard and fine across the plateau from Lame Deer to Busby. By the time we reached Crow Agency and I-90, it was 1:00 A.M. We'd covered a meager forty-two miles in an hour and a half. The events of the day flashed in and out of the mesmerizing whitewash of blizzard in the headlights. Finally, just west of Billings, the wind died and the air warmed. The temperature hovered around 32 degrees, and the light falling snow melted as it hit the pavement. Somehow the storm had skirted the interstate, but it would certainly push west toward the mountains. If we hurried, we could beat the front to the divide. Miraculously, Tom picked up his monologue right where he'd left it that afternoon, and I hoped he could keep talking. The wind was at our backs. The storm had arrived. It was going to be a long night.

As the car drone and Tom's voice and the occasional wind gust punctuated by snow flurry made counterpoint against the endless black of the sky, I tried to assimilate what had happened to me that day. My first experience with "Indian time." Alex Black Horse. Irene's nephew. Clearly, I had entered a world where the rules for social interaction sharply contrasted with those of the dominant culture. But more than that, I suspected that there was a deeper set of rules defining a truly different way of experiencing the world. I wondered if that way was common to all Cheyennes. After we stopped for gas in Laurel, I asked Tom about the interaction between Irene and her nephew. Why hadn't he answered her back?

"Well," he said, "part of it has to do with kinship. There are some relatives a Cheyenne man can't speak to directly. But it also has to do with their responses to conflict. It's generally considered rude to argue or answer back if someone confronts you, especially if it's a woman. In the old days a man was expected to be a good hunter and horse thief. If he wasn't, his wife and the other women would make a circle around him and bad-mouth him and sing nasty songs about him, generally humiliating him in front of everybody. And he had to take it in silence.

"It's the same in tribal council. Everyone is allowed to speak for as long as he wants to, and there is usually no comment made after a speech is given. They just think about it. If somebody is pissed off and attacks someone else personally, they don't argue. When it's finished, the one who got yelled at usually asks to be excused and then leaves the council. It's got its good and bad points."

Tom was quiet, and I wondered about Irene's nephew. If the rules of communal life still applied, even though the means for obeying those rules were gone, what kind of dilemma did that represent for a young man who was expected to care for his elders? And what would his recourse be if he failed those familial obligations? In the old days he could return to the hunt and make up for his shortcomings, but on the reservation, things were different. I wondered what Irene's nephew did after she scolded him and sent him back into the night.

We drove in silence for a long time. And then, somewhere outside Bozeman, in the middle of the Gallatin valley, the stormy night sky cleared and offered us stars and calm winds. We weren't fooled. The storm could close in again, and we still had the divide to cross. As the lights from Bozeman faded and we started the climb, I realized how much I had to learn. I found it difficult to reconcile my own feelings of shame about Indian-white relations in Montana with the generosity I'd received from Henry and Irene. As I learned later, Cheyennes are expected to give the best they have to their guests. It is the traditional way. Nevertheless, I wondered, given our history, how many Cheyenne couples would be as generous to a white guy with a camera. And how many white couples would have been so generous had our history been reversed? Would traditions of Christian charity hold as true as the Cheyenne traditions practiced by Henry and Irene? I wondered and watched the stars slowly disappear behind the storm.

As the snow came faster and we pressed on in silence through the waves of white that twisted across the road in front of us, I decided I wanted to know more. I wanted to return to Lame Deer.

And then the car was in a snow bank. As if in a dream, I had watched it happen like some odd phenomenon disconnected from me. The wind had graded the snow perfectly from the center of the road to the side and we'd been sucked into it without a struggle. We stepped out to survey the damage. The passenger side was buried up to the wheel wells. It was four in the morning. The interstate was deserted, and the fine snow was fast covering our tracks.

We were at the Continental Divide above Butte. Below, we could see street lights, and the Berkeley Pit mine, "the richest hole on earth," glowed like a frosted green jewel at the bottom of the bowl of the town. There was an odd, familiar stillness in this darkest part of the night, and we stood in it for a while trying to shake off the need for sleep. Silently, we both gauged the car's proximity to the edge of the canyon wall, and I, at least, considered how far down our demise might have occurred. Tom looked at me and raised his eyebrows. We shivered and heaved the car out of the drift.

It was not quite dawn when we stopped in Drummond for breakfast. By then I had abandoned soul-searching in favor of strong coffee. We still had fifty miles to go, but the storm seemed to have been confined east of the divide. The air was warmer and the snow on the road had turned to slush. After breakfast, Tom was driving but he wasn't talking; we were talked out. As the car droned on into daylight, the coffee failed and sleep caught me.

It was the kind of sleep that strikes quickly and plummets you into the deepest pit of mindlessness. And, just as violently as I was thrown down, the sound of a Kenworth's diesel pulling eighteen wheels snapped me into consciousness again. Each of those eighteen wheels was throwing a rooster tail of slush fifteen feet into the air, and we were awash in their wake. At the edge of my return to consciousness, Tom announced he was going to pass the truck.

Just as we pushed through the wall of ice-mud, the car spun 360 degrees and then slid sideways at fifty miles an hour atop a road skinned with glare ice. The Kenworth bore down on us, unable to slow or stop. Somehow the car faced forward again and Tom aimed it for the gully between the two bands of interstate. The snow trough gobbled up the car; the Kenworth passed and gave us a final dousing; and then there was a comforting silence, with just the sounds of the engine idling and our hearts pounding.

We kept that silence for a very long time. In the course of twenty-five hours we had spanned the state twice, most of that time in the car, and I was questioning the wisdom of the enterprise from a less than philosophical position. When I checked my camera bag for damage, I noted that I had exposed but one roll of film, and it was devoid of Cheyenne faces; even its latent landscapes were marginal in every way. Photographically, the trip had been a failure. And yet, as we got the car back on the interstate with the help of a sympathetic motorist and then began the ice marathon to Missoula at fifteen miles an hour, I knew I wanted to go back to Lame Deer, but I had no idea why.

A few days later, Henry called Tom and wondered if I would be coming to Lame Deer with him every month, and if I was, he wanted Tom and me to stay with him and Irene at their house. Tom relayed the request and looked hopeful.

"I have to go down every month for the writing project meetings," he said. "Sometimes I have to stay a week but it's usually just for the weekend. You might be able to do that photo project with the elders. I'm getting expense money for the project, so it won't cost you much. Irene really likes you."

I laughed and accepted the inevitable. Anyway, I'd already decided.

As I looked at the neat stack of photos on Irene's lap, I finally confronted Henry's face in death. The ravages of alcoholism were etched deeply there. He looked much older than fifty-five, and I tried to connect the face in the coffin with the one I'd seen on my first trip to Lame Deer. I tried to find some sequence of logic or fate that could span the distance between those faces. Most of that first trip had been like the Montana winter we drove through, beyond our control, beyond predictability. And just as certainly, in some incomprehensible way, all my journeys to Lame Deer had been deeply beyond my control, perilous and inevitable. But the face in the coffin registered a suffering impervious to anything as superficial as my poor attempts at fatalism. The face in the coffin revealed the map of Henry's story—his story, not mine, but one I'd been privileged, briefly, to share. It was a history I knew I would spend the rest of my life trying to understand.

2

Irene and I sat in the half-light and let our words come in and out of the silence in the way I'd learned to practice since that first night—grace of Alex Black Horse. And within the weave of our sound and silence my eyes scanned the room that had been the center of a second home for me. I couldn't look at the photos on her lap any more. Even so, it seemed that Henry's presence hovered in every corner. Over the course of many long nights in this room we had found and nurtured our friendship and had come to regard ourselves as family.

There was a longer silence, and then she said, "I'll make us some coffee."

"Coffee would be good," I said.

She got up and placed the pictures in the center of her chair. While she put the coffee on, I thought about kinship and the Cheyenne family and Spirit People.

It had been revelatory for me to learn that no Cheyenne child is ever without parents. The brothers of any child's father are also that child's fathers. The sisters of any child's mother are also that child's mothers. The generational consequence of kinship for the community is that everyone has a multiplicity of parents and grandparents, and so old age, like childhood, is free of any possibility of abandonment. It is in this way that Henry Tall Bull could claim the most famous Northern Cheyenne medicine man—White Bull, or Ice—as his grandfather, and in this way that Henry could feel the deepest connection to a world he'd never known.

Medicine men, or Spirit People, are said to have special powers. Spirit People are those rare individuals who, by natural inclination, have access to knowledge beyond the perceptions of others. Traditionally, Spirit People are healers, ceremonial priests, political and social consultants, clairvoyants, interpreters of dreams, guardians of tradition and stories, sorcerers, spokesmen for the chiefs, and community heralds. But the exercise of those powers depends upon unilateral recognition from all the clan societies in the tribe, because no council or ceremony can proceed without the sanction and heraldry of an officially designated medicine man.

Spirit People simply emerge and must be recognized. A Spirit Person can be male or female, but one officially recognized by all clans is usually a man. Most of the traditional stories about Spirit People are about men and emphasize their mystical powers.

Ice, Henry's great-grandfather, was most famous for his magic. On one occasion he instructed the young men of the tribe to bind and wrap him in rawhide thongs and place him at the bottom of a twelve-foot pit, which they then covered with a huge flat stone. Hours later, they returned and found the stone as they had placed it, but Ice was sitting on top of it. When they removed the stone, the rawhide ropes were still at the bottom of the pit, the knots and wrapping completely undisturbed.

It is said that Crazy Mule, another medicine man, killed three white soldiers from a distance of one mile by simply looking at them. As he stared, they became dizzy, stumbled, were paralyzed, and died. Crazy Mule said he had to use great caution when he looked at anyone. I didn't know about White Bull and Crazy Mule or their connection to Henry when he sat before me in his living room for a portrait. It was just as well.

It was my second trip to Lame Deer. Tom and I had arrived the night before and were greeted again with a feast, stories, and visitors. I was treated as the guest of honor by Irene, who gave me her daughter's bedroom for the night. In the morning, pancakes and eggs and bacon warmed the February chill. After breakfast, when I asked Henry to sit for me, he responded as if it was a foregone conclusion.

The light from the front window was ideal—midwinter light from an overcast sky, flat and uniform. I instinctively reached into the camera bag for my highlight enhancer, a small bottle of Johnson's baby oil. Henry stiffened a little when I explained and moved my moistened fingers toward his face. And then it was I who stiffened, suddenly hesitant within the profundity of the human touch. My coupled fingers, shocked by the softness of his skin, paused at the deep scar on his forehead, as if waiting for something—a question, asked and answered.

We talked easily through the sitting, but he suppressed his usual broad smile in an effort to cover his missing teeth. At last he relaxed and looked out the window while his vision turned inward, and what I had felt there moments earlier was there again as the shutter clicked—something complex and mysterious beneath the scar and behind his eyes that would find its way through the negative and into the portrait.

Afterward, Henry stood up, smiled secretively, made sure that Irene was within earshot, and said, "Would you like to go see my woman? You could take her picture too!" From the kitchen, a string of Cheyenne invective slashed at his laughter while I wobbled again in search of a response. "It's all right," he said. "She has a heart of stone!"

We drove north out of Lame Deer toward Colstrip. It was late morning, and as we passed Jimtown, the pyramid of empty bottles behind it flashed briefly in the sun. A magpie perched on the top fluttered its wings and fluffed itself while Tom and Henry debated the comparative height of the bottles and the roof peak.

Jimtown wasn't really a town. Rather, it was the first watering hole off the reservation and had pushed its accessibility right to the edge of the legal boundary: alcohol was prohibited on the reservation, but Jimtown was within walking distance of Lame Deer. Henry said he tended bar there once in a while. Judging from the pile of bottles, business was good.

We could still see the glint off the bottles when we left the pavement and entered the maze of dirt roads connecting all the local ranches with one another and with nothing at all. The conversation or, rather, Tom's monologue had turned to Cheyenne warriors. It was Henry's favorite topic because the Cheyenne warriors, while still free on the plains, had been known to all as the ones who did not fear death.

There were only two ways for a Cheyenne soldier to win honor in battle: to survive untouched, having counted coup (struck first) or killed the enemy, or to die in a full frontal assault. To be wounded or captured was dishonorable, evidence that the warrior's medicine had failed. Therefore, every warrior went into battle expecting to die. His goal was to die with honor for his family and his people. And so he prepared his medicine, sang his own funeral songs, said goodbye to his family, and, when it was time, charged the enemy with impunity. If he survived, he was surprised.

The warrior's beliefs about death were confirmed on the battlefield as a tactical maneuver by the suicide warriors or suicide boys. When the opposing forces faced each other, the Cheyenne offense was sometimes initiated by those who had taken the vow of suicide. The vow was usually made for personal reasons: revenge, illness, unhappiness, a failed love affair, or sometimes depression over a life no longer bearable. Whatever the reason, suicide in battle was an honorable way to die.

When it was time, the suicide warriors stripped themselves naked, charged the enemy lines on unbridled mounts, and assaulted them with bare hands, feet, and teeth until their astonished foes killed them. The tactic never failed to unnerve the enemy, who now understood with certainty that the Cheyennes were not afraid to die. And so the successive Cheyenne assaults were typically devastating.

Tom talked, and I was lost in my own visions of plains warriors and the image of the suicide warriors. Suddenly I felt the scar again beneath my fingertips and saw Henry's face again, bathed in winter light. My reveries were so complete, I didn't see Henry's sandstone woman come into view until he reached from the back seat and nudged me into consciousness.

"There she is—isn't she beautiful?!" I stared at the sandstone hill in front of us and searched in vain for her while Tom slowed the car. Suddenly, the jagged outcropping assumed the profile of a woman. There was "Henry's woman," and she was impressive. Her sandstone profile was about ninety feet above the plain and proudly faced the vast expanse. But like the Egyptian Sphinx she had been the merciless victim of target practice, and her once aquiline nose was shattered beyond recognition. Nonetheless, her most feminine attribute, an enormous bosom, was well preserved and the obvious object of Henry's admiration. Beyond her physical charms, however, Henry loved her because she was the product of erosion, a woman of stone born of entropy.

When I stepped out of the car, camera bag in hand, he innocently queried, "You gonna put baby oil on that too?"

Amid their laughter, Tom suggested we return to Lame Deer for ladders, buckets, and mops! I set up the tripod and view camera to immortalize Henry's woman. And with that record, a deeper precedent was set.

We knew this was the first of many sorties that would carry us deep into the heart of the great plains. Out there we would seek power spots and walk the ground of our ancestors in search of their memories, their hopes, and their failed dreams. I knew we would do all that and more when I turned away from Henry's sandstone woman and saw him waiting in the car, looking at me.

In that moment I felt as though Henry *saw* me, recognized those things in me that I guarded so carefully: my ambivalence and my hubris about who I thought I was (fool? artist?), my love of landscapes, and my vulnerability and fear that my incompetence would show. And when he looked at me, I felt that it did show. But whatever he saw, it clearly amused him in the way men are amused when they've made the decision to be friends. I looked back at him and knew we were going to be friends.

Back in Lame Deer, as we parked in front of Henry's house again, Tom suggested we visit Grover Wolf Voice. He and Grover had become friends while Tom lived on the reservation, and Tom was sure he would sit for a portrait.

Tom had taken a deep interest in Grover's flutemaking, and so Grover had enlisted him and his car in the endless search for the perfect cedar tree—a tree that could be found only offroad, of course. Equally certain were both the futility and the hazards of the quest as they bounced up and down coulees and along the edges of buttes.

Grover, in his mid-eighties, was the last of the Cheyenne flutemakers. Although always at work on flutes and in need of materials, he clearly enjoyed getting Tom to drive him up and down the hills more than actually finding trees. Cedar was the traditional material, scarce on the reservation and therefore highly prized. But Grover liked to confess that the best-sounding flute he'd ever made came from a section of old aluminum bicycle frame that he plugged and wrapped in rawhide. He and Tom never actually found that perfect tree. Nevertheless, seasoned cedar logs, quartersawn and ready for carving, were always stacked on Grover's front porch.

Visiting Grover each month was an imperative for Tom, and given the speed of reservation gossip, by the time we got back to

Henry's it was certain that Grover not only knew we were in town; he was expecting us, and there was still enough afternoon light for another portrait.

We said goodbye to Henry in his front yard. As the door closed behind him and we turned toward our car, John Woodenlegs drove up. Stepping out, he greeted Tom warmly over the top of his car and invited him to the prayer meeting that night. Then, after a thoughtful pause and a smile, he invited me as well. Without knowing what I'd agreed to attend, I readily assented and thanked him. He offered an ambiguous clue as he slid back into his car: "Not one-hour church — pray all night."

On the way to Grover's house, Tom enlightened me. John Woodenlegs was a modern religious leader who sustained the ancient tradition of medicine men and ceremonial priests. He had been president of the Native American Church since 1948 and had been instrumental in achieving federal sanction for the use of peyote as an integral part of the ceremony. His efforts also helped win official recognition for the Native American Church as a legitimate religion, thereby ending nearly a century of religious persecution. An invitation to a peyote ceremony from John Woodenlegs was indeed an honor.

The significance of the invitation, however, was quickly obscured by the perils of Lame Deer streets in midwinter thaw, streets whose summer hardpan of red clay had been transformed into bottomless canyons of viscous blood-black slush. We left the car on a shallow section of the road and picked our way through the muck toward the house. As expected, Grover was standing on the porch, waiting to greet us.

He leaned easily on one crutch. His massive frame, even stooping, was well over six-foot-five and crowded the porch. His legs were bowed and twisted from rheumatoid arthritis. Although nagged by chronic pain, Grover, like Irene Tall Bull, still knew how to live the good life. His crutches somehow disappeared at powwows so that he could dance with the best of them.

His broad face beamed as we struggled through the mud toward the porch. And that face, almost flat, with high cheek bones and broad mouth, reflected his mixed heritage: part Cheyenne, part Gros-Ventre. The latter implied kinship with the Crows, and since the Crows are ancient Cheyenne rivals, Grover alternately denied the connection or devilishly promoted it, depending on the

sensitivities of those he happened to encounter. He had a reputation for his wicked sense of humor, and his barbed one-liners, always well timed and deadly, were fast becoming folklore. But beyond everything else, Grover had been a peyote man since 1927.

About twenty feet from the porch we found solid ground again
and paused while Grover and Tom exchanged greetings. Grover
had miscalled him "Mr. West" from the beginning, and Tom was
never sure whether he persisted in it out of habit or if there was
some embedded, ambiguous joke that Grover expected him to get.
I scraped the mud off my shoes and surveyed the house.

It was of Montana homesteader vintage, 1920s or thereabouts,
the kind Honyockers built quickly before a second bad winter had
to be endured but built stout and basic, with room for the improvements that none of those houses ever seemed to acquire. The
steep roof was corrugated metal over original shingles and skip-
sheathing and could shed any amount of snow. The original cedar
clapboard siding remained, black-gold from two generations of
weathering, though several boards had fallen away and the tar-
paper undercoat billowed slightly in the February wind. The two
windows flanking the porch were covered with heavy plastic secured by lath board—makeshift storm windows that buffered the
wind and covered the cracked panes that marred each frame. The
porch listed heavily to one side yet managed to support a cord of
firewood as well as Grover's stash of cedar for flutes. The entire
structure was at the crest of a slight rise above the road and was
supported by stone footings, posts, and joists skirted with broad
cedar planks to mitigate the draft beneath the floor. As a period
piece its historical reference was double, representing at once the
homesteaders and one stage in the architectural evolution of reservation housing—from tipi to log cabin to Honyocker ranch house
to the California pre-fab. Wisps of wood smoke from the galvanized stack drifted down over the porch roof and hovered briefly
just above the ground in the front yard.

The yard itself was unbounded, its beige summer coat of prairie
grass matted down, clotted with mud and some remaining January
snow. In the center a fifty-gallon drum contained smoldering
garbage and was surrounded by a collection of nondescript non-
combustibles. Two car bodies of 1940s and 1950s vintage stood
partially buried in the ground, the earth slowly absorbing them
year by year. Beyond the trash pile, in the shelter of a small group

of cottonwoods, an outhouse afforded an ample view of Lame Deer
and the landscape beyond. The open door revealed two thrones,
flanked on one side by a stack of catalogues and on the other by
a larger stack of newspapers—each offering both reading and
hygienic material.

The air was warm around us, the kind that comes at the end of
one storm and waits for another—dry, thin as a bird's bone.
Grover's immense hand was soft around mine. I shall never forget
that handshake, the gentle clasp and release—strength felt after it
was gone. And I remember climbing the three steps to the porch to
enter the house. And I remember, as we stepped inside, touching
the paint-peeled door.

Inside the kitchen we were welcomed twice by the dry, even
warmth from the well-damped Majestic stove and the palatable
smell of fresh coffee. Grover's granddaughter turned away from us
on a shy smile and waited for us to pass into the next room, where
she would serve the coffee in heavy white restaurant cups. When
Grover went by, her slight frame seemed even smaller by compari-
son. She leaned lightly on palms turned inward at the edge of a
sink in which stood two freshly pumped buckets of well water; beneath it was a larger bucket to catch the waste. To her left a small
trestle table supported the large blue enamel coffeepot wrapped in
a heavy towel. Next was a refrigerator older than the cars in the
yard, and beyond it a doorway to a darkened room. In the center of
the kitchen a small wooden dining table still damp from scrubbing
was graced by an eagle feather in a bud vase. Above her head, two
shelves held three plates, two enameled cups that matched the pot,
and a small selection of generic staples: salt, flour, oatmeal, beans.
To her right was the doorway to the next room. Above us all, a
single light bulb hung from the ceiling by its braided cord. She
seemed to stand directly beneath it with her weight on her left foot,
her head tilted slightly to the right. She was wearing fairly new
moccasins, the kind that extend well up the calf. Her print dress
was faded, and a flour-sack dish towel was draped unevenly over
her right shoulder. Grover spoke softly to her in Cheyenne as he
passed. She didn't answer but stepped to her left as we followed
him into the next room.

This was the sitting room, and it doubled as his bedroom (the
official one to the left of the kitchen being given to his granddaughter). In this room too was centered a single suspended light

bulb. The front window faced its opposite in the back wall, and both cast light filtered through plastic toward the center of the room. Between, the windowless plastered side wall was a faded green, stained by wood smoke and water marks that chronicled the roof's history of failure against spring and summer cloudbursts. The plaster had fallen away in a few places and showed the lath beneath. But for three wooden kitchen chairs of unspecified origin and the single brass-framed bed, the room was without appointments. In the shadow where the light of the opposing windows failed to meet, a small rectangle a shade paler than the rest of the wall was punctuated by a single nail near the top, the memory of a picture once hung there.

Grover sat on the edge of the bed and propped his crutches against the brass rail at its foot. Beneath it were two steamer trunks which I assumed held his clothing, for there were no closets or shelves in the room. Tom and I sat on two of the chairs and sipped hot coffee. I looked down at the fir plank floor. The small mud clods from our shoes stood out against its well-worn silvered surface, which was washed as clean as the kitchen table.

There was a brief stillness, and then Tom mentioned that John Woodenlegs had invited us to the peyote meeting. Tom offered to take Grover. Grover responded with his favorite story about his grandfather, who had made an art form of ecumenical church attendance in the early days of the reservation. He managed to attend all the white man's churches on a scheduled basis, sometimes getting to several on a single Sunday. Once, a hopeful Catholic priest, who had observed the old man's ways for a few weeks and thought he was church shopping, asked which church he preferred. The old man quickly replied, "Pentecostal." When the disappointed priest asked why, grandfather replied that they simply had the best food. It seems his routine was regulated by the after-church coffee hour and potluck schedule from one denomination to the next. He did confess that the Methodists ran a close second but that their potluck was only once a month.

We laughed quietly beneath his talk, and then Tom mentioned that John Woodenlegs was putting up the meeting to bless and celebrate the completion of the new octagonal structure he had built especially for peyote meetings; it would be warmer in winter and hold more people. Grover smiled his wicked smile and grunted, "Prayer meetings are in tipis. When will you come pick me up?"

We laughed again about Indian time, and then the talk turned to me and pictures. And then, with unexpected swiftness, Grover reached beneath the bed, pulled out a steamer trunk, and removed a large, navy blue robe with bright red trim. It was his peyote robe, and with its appearance the air was instantly clotted with the pungent aroma of sage.

Tom couldn't resist. "It smells like a giant peyote, Grover!" and they both laughed while I took the camera and light meter from my bag and made a quick reading.

Tom talked about peyote meetings past, all recorded in the smell of the robe, while I watched Grover prepare. He unfolded the robe slowly, his immense hands almost caressing the surface as he smoothed it. And as he did, a deep reverence moved through the lines in his face and softened them. He carefully draped the robe around his shoulders and at last removed his glasses, whose thickness had all but obscured his eyes. A large finger reached out from beneath the robe to straighten the line of red trim at the front.

He was ready. He presented himself as he wanted to be known, a man who has taken the peyote road. Suddenly there was no house, no yard, no reservation. Just me and Tom and Grover Wolf Voice, peyote man. And finally—just Grover in the cross light, alone on the ground glass.

That day we left Grover as we had found him, standing on the front porch, leaning on one crutch. And after that day, visiting the reservation each month meant visiting Grover each month. Each month our routine was the same. Grover greeted us from the porch, always addressed Tom as Mr. West, and then took us to his sitting room, where he sat on the bed, pulled out the steamer trunk, and sorted through the orderly stack of ceremonial material and clothing to find his deer-bone pipe and sack of tobacco. Each time, we smoked quietly, passing the pipe around to afford an equal amount to each of us. The mixture, however, of two parts kinnickinnick plus one part Bull Durham never failed to give me a skyrocketing fifteen-second buzz that made Grover and the faded green wall behind him sparkle and dance. And then it was over and he'd put the pipe away, and I would give him a print from the last time, and he would rebuke me: "Cheyenne men don't have white hair!—have black hair! Do you have another one from last time? I gave it to my grandson."

Our monthly "smoke" echoed the formal Pipe Ceremony, which is serious business. In that ceremony, promises are made—promises that, when "smoked on," must be kept, for the promises within the Pipe Ceremony are about reciprocity. If a young man decides to dance in the Sun Dance, he must smoke the Medicine Pipe with his sponsor so that each can make a vow: the young man, to fast and dance for four days; the sponsor, to prepare him and guide him through the ceremony. The smoke is, of course, the vow itself, rising upward to Ma'heo'o, the Heavenly Father.

No vows as such were taken between Grover and Tom and me, but an unspoken promise was made. We smoked on what each visit and the portrait sittings represented. We smoked to set the context, the sacred space for each visit. Finally, "smoking on it" was necessary because Grover was fully aware of his position.

Tom was aware of it too. As their friendship developed during Tom's residence on the reservation, Tom had taken an archival interest in Grover's art. One summer, he tried to document Grover's flutemaking process. He made some photographs and recorded some flute songs. But for Grover, the problems were beyond the capabilities of tape recorders.

The tradition of flute playing and flutemaking as it had been passed to him from his ancestors could easily die with him, and he often worried because he had no apprentices. All the traditional flute songs, like the craft of carving and tuning the instrument, resided in him and him alone. But the essence of that tradition was resident in his behavior, his style as a player, which could not be captured in a recording. All this and the many cultural references that could emerge only over the course of a long and intimate apprenticeship were finally what was at stake.

Grover knew that, and so he always made himself available to give presentations, especially to Cheyenne schoolchildren. There his artistry as a player and storyteller exemplified the ancient medicine embodied in the flute. And that medicine was used for courting.

When an amorous young man courted his sweetheart in the old days, he sat all night on a hill near her tipi and played the courting songs. If he played elegantly enough to release the flute's medicine, she would be unable to resist. Overcome by the power of the song she would be compelled to sneak out and meet him. If his playing and love were true, the flute's medicine would literally fly out of the instrument as sparks of fire, embers of love, shooting stars in the night.

Although the children always loved the part about the sparks, Grover usually amended it: "We don't need the sparks anymore— now that we have mini-skirts!"

Grover told it all to me the first time we smoked and he played the flute and we laughed. But underneath our laughter, in the echo of the song and the smoke, it was as if I were sitting next to the last human in my white culture who could read musical notation and play the music of Bach and Chopin and all the rest, knowing that with his passing an entire modality of exquisite human thought would be relegated to oblivion. It could be no less telling for any Cheyenne person who sat with Grover. The finality of extinction is eternal. When a culture dies, it never comes back.

Each time we left him, my sense of the finite sharpened. But each time we returned and found him still there, still full of wicked humor and still glad to see us, denial was just as easy. No one is really prepared to confront the "last" of anything, especially those of us who come from worlds where abundance of everything precludes the possibility of nothingness. Beyond any sense of the finite, Grover and Tom and I didn't believe that the Cheyenne flute and its songs would end with him because we had "smoked on it" and the promise was made, and so there was hope.

Night comes swiftly in February on the plains, and when we got back to Henry's house it was very dark beneath clouds and a new moon. Irene was alone and ambiguous about Henry's whereabouts. When she heard that we were going to the prayer meeting, she beamed and extolled the virtues of peyote as a curative for her arthritis. Indeed, she claimed that the mobility she still had was due to the power of the cactus.

We assured her that we'd get supper on our own and excused ourselves. Tom was anxious to "prep" me for the long night ahead, and the first step in his regimen was to consume great quantities of food at the Lame Deer Cafe as a buffer against the nausea and vomiting that peyote offered as its first steps toward enlightenment. He insisted that his method, contradictory as it seemed, really did work.

Irene insisted we stop by before we returned to Missoula. She wanted a report. She wanted me to like peyote.

Irene and I sat facing each other in her living room, safe within the shaded late morning light. I looked at her twisted hands as they gently squared the stack of Polaroids on her lap and was suddenly aware that I was talking about peyote meetings. I was reminding her about my first peyote meeting, the one I had been invited to by John Woodenlegs, and I was telling her how he believed that the peyote medicine was the only sure way for the Cheyenne people to be rid of alcoholism. She nodded, and in the silence after I said that, she looked hard at the picture on top of the stack. We both knew that we were thinking about the man in the coffin and what we couldn't say. And then she looked up again, past me into the shadows. I started telling her about that first meeting, and it was as if I were experiencing it all again, at that moment, within the shade of her living room.

Once again I am there—with Tom—and he's telling me about peyote meetings.

Once again I am sitting in the Lame Deer Cafe with Tom, and I am acutely aware of every detail. I can hear the forced air heater in the far upper corner of the room wheeze as it fights the draft that is everywhere. I can smell the grill while we wait for our dinner.

When it comes, I confront a plate of fried potatoes and gravy and a steak whose toughness adds a new dimension to the notion of free-range meat. Tom and I chew hard and discuss the church and its history. I've already read Weston La Barre's treatise on the "peyote cult," as he called it, and so I have some general knowledge about the religion.

I know that peyote is ancient medicine and was used extensively by North American natives long before Columbus. I know there are surviving Aztec codices that describe peyote as a remarkable plant capable of producing visions. The Aztec priests included it regularly in ceremonies as an offering, and their descendants—the Yaqui, Otomi, and Tarahumare—have continued the ceremonial use of the cactus. But the peyote ceremony as it is practiced now began with the healing experience of the Comanche Quanah Parker, in the mid-1880s.

I know Parker's story and how he was saved from death by the Tarahumare medicine woman who cured his fevered coma with massive doses of peyote tea. Parker went on to establish the peyote way and preach about its medicine. Tom mentions that the Ghost Dance, a more messianic movement, appeared about that same time; he says that Wovoka, the Payute messiah, offered the dance as the way to renew the land, to bring back the buffalo, and, finally, to bring about the destruction of the white man in a great flood.

We struggle some more with our T-bones while the talk turns to Porcupine, a Northern Cheyenne medicine man who made a pilgrimage to Pyramid Lake, Nevada, in 1889 and saw the messiah, Wovoka. Porcupine was converted and brought the Ghost Dance to Montana. That same year, Leonard Tyler, a Southern Cheyenne, came to Lame Deer to preach the gospel of the peyote religion. Tom thought that both movements represented a profound response to the collapse of the buffalo culture and all the ceremonies attached to it. In the wake of catastrophe many sought relief in the promise of the messiah.

Eventually, the Cheyennes settled into religious practices that suited their needs. Some became devout members of the various Christian sects. Some continued traditional practice as best they could, often secretly, since many ceremonies were prohibited by the BIA. The Ghost Dance disappeared following the death of Sitting Bull and the massacre at Wounded Knee. Porcupine, after serving time in the Lame Deer jail for ghost-dancing, stopped preaching about it. And so the peyote religion, as a blend of Christian and traditional practice, eventually found its niche within a deeply religious society.

Suddenly it's eight o'clock and time to go pick up Grover. On the way, Tom assures me that I will be fine and welcomed at the meeting because, John Woodenlegs's invitation notwithstanding, it is principle within the peyote way that anyone who comes through the tipi door is welcome.

We arrive at Grover's house, and Tom aims the headlights at the front porch to light our way. We leave the engine running and the heater blasting—a small comfort for Grover's arthritic joints. Once we get to the porch we peer through the glass in the door. Grover is standing near the entrance to the sitting room, his peyote robe draped unevenly around his shoulders. He sees us and beckons. We step inside and wait while he finishes instructions to his granddaughter, who is on her knees with a skinning knife poised above a freshly killed and gutted deer carcass splayed on the floor in front of her. She nods respectfully as his instructions roll forth. He pauses briefly to greet us and then backs out of the room and the house, guiding us out backward while continuing the lecture that ends several seconds after the door is shut. I feel his strength when he grabs my arm to steady himself as we descend the porch steps and move through the glare of the headlights to the car.

When we arrive at John Woodenlegs's place, his new octagonal building seems to float in the darkness. The door is open, and the light from within spills out and absorbs the last few people as they enter. We are too late to hear John, who is Road Chief for the meeting, say the prayers at the four cardinal directions outside and then offer his blessings at the entrance. Tom and I ease Grover out of the car and follow him to the door. He's left his crutches at home, and his balance seems remarkably improved. By the time he reaches the entrance he is walking easily, and his stoop is gone.

At the doorway the Fireman, or keeper of the fire, holds the canvas flap back with one arm and lets us step forward into the room. Each must wait for the Road Chief's greeting and permission to enter. After Grover, I step over the threshold.

Directly in front of me is the fire. It is amply stoked with cottonwood and is vented by a metal cowling and smokestack that substitute for the traditional vent flap of a tipi. Aside from its practical value, the fire is the symbolic offering of the Fireman, who will extract coals from it throughout the night and shape them into a large glowing thunderbird.

The coals that will become the thunderbird are drawn away from the door toward the sand-crescent altar. It is about four inches high at the center and is beveled into the shape of a waxing crescent moon about four feet in length. The Chief Peyote, a large ceramic replica of the cactus, adorns the center of the altar.

Against the wall directly opposite the door sits the Road Chief. To his right is his drummer, who holds the ceremonial wand and gourd. To his left is the Cedar Man, or keeper of the incense. He holds a large eagle-feather fan and a rawhide bag containing cedar shavings. He will anoint all those who pray with cedar smoke from the fire by sprinkling the shavings onto the thunderbird and directing the smoke with the fan over their bodies. The smoke will carry their prayers to Ma'heo'o. Centered in the triangle formed by the three of them is the peyote drum.

My eyes travel slowly from the fire to the altar and the Chief Peyote and then find the face of John Woodenlegs. He smiles at me. "Welcome—come in!" I move clockwise around the circle and find the next available space. I'm grateful. I'll be sitting next to Grover.

John begins the opening prayers as the Fireman removes a cottonwood branch from the fire. He rolls a cigarette and lights it with the smoldering end. He passes the tobacco sack and papers to his left and then the branch. John's prayer flows above it all on the same soft rhythmic cadence that Alex Black Horse spoke in conversation that first night. How small is the difference between the sound of that conversation and this prayer.

John prays all the while that each of us is smoking. After we finish our cigarettes, we hold the butts until the prayers are finished. Then, one at a time, we place the tobacco offering on the sand-crescent altar. Grover hands his to me so he won't have to get up. I place them carefully, side by side, near the south tip of the sand moon and then look up at the doorway. It faces east where the sun will rise, and I am suddenly aware that it will be our primary task to share this long night. Through the concerted effort of the faithful, the sun will rise.

The opening prayers are finished, and John's drummer, Francis Black Horse, is preparing the drum for the opening round of songs. Tom says he is the best drummer on the reservation. Although he is well past sixty years, his hair is still jet black and his wiry frame quite muscular. He handles the drum carefully, each movement anchored in ceremonial history.

The drum is of cast metal. In the early days, peyote drums were made from cast-iron cooking pots, the ten-quart variety with four small feet at the perimeter of the bottom. Contemporary drums are usually cast or spun aluminum. The drumhead is well tanned deerskin which is soaked in water, then wrapped tightly around the drum and secured with rawhide thongs. The metal feet serve as guides and anchors. Inside the drum is a small quantity of water mixed with ashes from a previous prayer meeting. In this way the sound of the drum and the song are imbued with the medicine— the present infused with the past.

John holds the wand and rattle while Francis ties and reties the drumhead. At last he is satisfied and with his left hand holds the drum at an angle on the ground. In his right hand is the mallet, a slender wooden rod, wrapped in his fingers and held against the palm. He pushes his left thumb into the drum head to tighten the skin as his right hand begins a slow beat that quickly accelerates to a throbbing two-hundred beats per minute. It is a sound like no other I've ever heard: a full-throated tenor, resonant with the aspect of water, hollow as the sound of stones dropped into a deep pool—urgent as the wind.

John holds the wand straight and still while its eagle feather tresses shimmer in the drumbeat. His face smoothes, his eyes close, the rattle in his hand begins to echo the pulse of the drum, and then the song is there. It is from him and everywhere at once. It is suspended above us all inside an eagle's gyre until it strains against the pull of the earth and descends the spiral rapidly, descends and then hovers inches above the ground where the drumbeat awaits, pauses and then leaps back to the heights again, only to repeat again and again its soaring and its descending four times four times until the drum holds it to the ground and there is silence.

Francis adjusts the drum. And then the songs find us again as they will all night. Four cycles of four sets of songs represent the four cardinal directions and the four spirits that inhabit them, the four seasons of the earth, and the four sacred arrows, Sweet Medicine's gift to the people. Yet all of them are invocations to Ma'heo'o, the Heavenly Father, Jesus Christ, God. They are invocations to the same God of all men, invocations for help, healing, peace, and well-being. All of them will follow the drum, gourd, and wand around the circle, each participant singing or drumming or listening as his or her needs dictate. All of them will carry us through the night.

I am lost in the songs and the firelight, and so I don't see the Fireman begin the first serving of the sacred plant. It comes in several forms. First, dried and shredded strands are buffed between the palms, then rubbed on the upper torso and placed in a shirt pocket. The hands, at last, are held out and up with palms toward the fire. Next comes the tea, followed by peyote ground into powder, then powder moistened into a paste, then whole cactus buttons, and at last a mason jar full of a mixture of tea, powder, and shredded cactus affectionately called peyote gravy. After this first ceremonial communion, the medicine is available on request. In deference to John, who watches me with hopeful interest, I have eaten some of each serving, including one whole button, and now I am struggling against the waves of nausea that rise within me and drench my brow with sweat.

And then, just at the moment when I'm sure I will be overwhelmed by sickness, I am calm. Inside the lull between rounds of song I am calm, and I know I am at the threshold of the peyote road. John invites me to sit with him. He hands me his personal peyote rattle. It is a beautiful gourd with a hardwood handle, smooth and glowing from years of contact with his hand. He shows me the rhythm with his clenched fist in the air. I try a few tentative shakes. He gently places his open palm on the gourd to silence it.

And then I'm looking across the altar into the fire and listening to John Woodenlegs explain what it means to follow a certain road.

"A road is a path that shows you the rules for how to conduct your life. If you get medicine from a coyote, you are following the coyote's road. If you take peyote medicine, you are following the peyote road. If you take the medicine and follow the road, then everything changes. You shouldn't mix roads. Cheyennes believe it's not good to mix medicines."

Across the altar I can see that this road begins with transformations. The altar is the new waxing moon that must attain fullness. The ashes of the fire become the thunderbird. Medicine transforms body and spirit. The night is transformed by drum and song into dawn while individuals become a community whose hopes, dreams, and fears are carried upward through the night into the sunrise on the smoke of prayer.

I hand John's rattle back to him and thank him and return to my place next to Grover, where I follow his steady gaze into the firelight. Soon my eyes are fixed on the glowing heat waves in the metal cowling that gathers the smoke from the flames.

"I think that's George Custer's stove!"

Grover had leaned into me and nudged my elbow with his as he said it. I am startled and astonished. I can't believe he said that, and I scan the circle for response. There is none, especially from John, for whom the comment was clearly intended. Grover's disapproval of "modern improvements" on the ceremony is lost on no one, and yet everyone holds very still after he says it—everyone except the woman directly across the circle from me, whose hand moves quickly to cover a smile and suppress a giggle. Tom coughs on his own laughter as John begins the midnight prayers and the call for water. Grover looks straight ahead but nudges me once more with his elbow to make sure I got the joke, while the Fireman holds the door flap open for the Water Woman.

She is here to remind us of the Tarahumare medicine woman, called the Curandera, who healed Quanah Parker with peyote. She kneels in front of the fire and altar and places the pail of water before her. John prays aloud over the silent company as each of us, in turn, drinks from the enameled dipper. The water is cool and sweet. The prayers end as she herself at last drinks and takes her leave.

In the silence after prayer, Grover nudges me again and asks me to help him stand. He has been immobile all this time, like a purple butte covered with snow. Others around the circle have asked to go out, and as I stand, I can feel the medicine working in me.

While I watch Grover move around the circle to the door, I continue to rise, like Alice in Wonderland, until my head and torso arch along the pitch of the ceiling; below, I see the entire circle, the tops of their heads, the fire, the thunderbird. I am moving now, and the circle moves with me. Somehow I shrink again and pass through the door into the clear and frozen night.

I stand inside the starlight and offer cigarettes to three Cheyenne men, and we smoke and face the cardinal directions of the universe and speak curtly about the cold. The drum and song rise up again, filling the spaces in our talk until they go back inside and I am alone. I can feel the movement of the earth beneath my feet. I can see the entire canopy of stars moving too, in opposition to me and the earth, and I can feel the galaxy spinning slowly inside my body. Above the peak of the roof and the thin line of smoke is a sliver of moon. Ice blue, minute in the distance, it is the fixed center of our collective motion. As I turn toward the door again I am very much aware of the absence of my feet. But the songs—and the drum—carry me inside.

Inside, the house is filled with smoke, and I am seized by the aroma of cedar and sage as the Cedar Man fans the prayers upward to Ma'heo'o. And then a young man, more boy than man, asks to pray. John beckons to him, and he moves to the northwest tip of the altar. He kneels down on one knee while a peyote robe is draped around his shoulders, and John prepares the smoke: a long cigarette of tobacco and dried peyote. The Cedar Man casts the shavings over the coals of the thunderbird, and the smoke rises and is

caught by the eagle feathers and is wrapped around the boy who
smokes and speaks of the father he's never known. He speaks of
the father who left him so long ago and who died so far away. He
weeps and smokes and prays for those in his family still caught in
the death spin of alcohol, and as he prays in English, John's voice
echoes his prayers in Cheyenne; both are inside the cedar smoke
rising until the words have pushed time away and the boy rises
again, his face wet and unified. He returns to the circle where his
eyes, cleansed by medicine and tears, find their way back to the
firelight.

My eyes follow his into the coals, and I am four years old. I know
I am four years old, and at the same time I know I'm a grown man
sitting next to Grover in front of the fire. I know I am four because
I can't go to kindergarten because you have to be five to go and I'm
not. I'm standing by my mom in front of the candy counter in
Dixon's store and I want some candy but I can't decide and my
mom says I should hurry up because I'm taking too long. All I can
see are the cinnamon bears and I don't want them. I want my mom
to pick me up so I can see what's on top. I think I hear something
behind me, so I let go of my mom's hand and turn around to see.

I look down at the biggest, most beautiful cowboy boots I've
ever seen. My eyes move quickly up the slender legs rising out of
the boots, pause at the large silver belt buckle, then scan the flow-
ered, pearl-buttoned cowboy shirt and halt abruptly at the sight of
very long, very black braids. My eyes move slowly from the braids
across the broad bronze face and are suddenly transfixed by the
even blacker eyes that stare deeply into mine.

"An Indian!"

I can't believe it is my voice that said it. It was so loud and the
store is so quiet now. I'm reaching for my mom's hand but I can't
find it. I start to call to her, but my ear hurts, and she's pulling it and
me out the door. She doesn't let go until we're on the sidewalk.

"What's the matter with you anyway!"

I don't know; I want to ask her if it was a real Indian, but I don't
because I know she's mad at me. I turn around and look back at the
store but all I can see is the still fall of midwinter snow and the playground full of children moving in and out of giant snow feathers
that cling to eyelashes and noses. I can see Jim through the snow.
He's littler than me, but we're both in Miss Krause's first grade
room. His skin is only light brown, but I know he's an Indian kid.

He never talks to anybody, and if you ask him something, he just shakes his head.

The snowflakes are falling faster, and its hard to see him and the snow is covering our feet. My fingers sting inside my mittens. I got them soaked and now my fingers hurt. It's getting colder and I can see my breath push the snowflakes away from my face. Jim isn't wearing a hat or a coat, and he hasn't any mittens. His flannel shirt is missing a button at the top, and his corduroy pants are ragged at the cuffs. The pants are too short for him, and I can see his bare ankles. He doesn't have any socks on. I ask if he's cold, but he just makes a tiny smile and shrugs and shakes his head.

I can't see Jim anymore, just snow, and so I turn around and look through the basement windows into the cafeteria. The Indian kids are all lined up for lunch. They look up at me through the windows, but we don't know each other. I can hear kids yelling behind me. The Indian kids are lined up against the wall and the other kids are in front of them. They're yelling back and forth—"We were here first!" The bell rings and we all run inside.

After recess, Miss Krause lines us up so we can go to the library. I like to go because we have to go up the stairs and through the tunnel to the new building. It's fun going through a tunnel that's up in the air. Just before we get there, we pass another room. There's no one but Indian kids in there. One boy with really dark skin and really black hair looks out the door, but his eyes don't see me. His eyes are black too—like the braided man in Dixon's store. I remember his eyes and I stop and stare at the boy in the room. Everybody behind me stumbles and bumps into each other and starts pushing, and Miss Krause pulls me out of line and tells me it's rude to stare. But the boy in the room doesn't move even when I look at him again. His eyes don't move either.

And then nothing moves as the gray late afternoon light through the lace curtain on the back door holds me still. I'm standing there in my snow puddles just inside the door. My mom carefully unwinds my frozen muffler and mittens. She holds my red chilled hands between hers and rubs and blows them warm. We say words to each other in the near darkness of the kitchen.

"Were the Indians here first?"

"Yes they were."

"Oh . . ."

Underneath our words there is a drum sound and a song and then I can't see my mom anymore. All I can see is Robert Falcon. I'm standing next to the teacher's desk and I can see him sitting in his desk where he always sits next to the door. He never looks up. He just plays with his pencil and stares at his hands while he does it. I'm staring at him while the teacher is talking to me. She says I'm the best at long division and so I have to help Robert with his. She says if I help him I won't have to do any more long division problems 'cause I can do them very well. She says that since the Indian kids are with us now we have to help them 'cause they're behind. Robert never answers her when she talks to him, and she gets mad but tries not to show it. Maybe she thinks I can do better with him. I think I can. If you're good at arithmetic it means you're really smart.

I'm sitting next to him now and I don't feel so smart anymore. He looks at me and I feel like he wants to pick a fight. And then he looks away. He looks down at his paper and plays with his pencil the way he always does. I look at the paper. There's nothing on it. He hasn't written anything, not even his name. I ask him if he can write the first problem and he just shrugs and slumps in his chair. I look at the teacher. She sees me looking but pretends not to notice. I look at him again and now I know. He doesn't know anything about arithmetic at all. He doesn't know what I'm talking about. He looks at me again and I see that he's ashamed. I freeze inside the blackness of his eyes. The bell rings, and we all wait for the teacher to say we can go home. Robert is the first one out the door.

I don't get up but turn my head to look at the teacher again. I can only see Grover's eyes. He smiles at me: "Peyote—good medicine." The man next to me nudges my arm and hands me a spoon and a cup filled with warm kernel corn. I look up into the morning light that spills through the doorway and covers the Water Woman, who kneels in the center of the room. Large enamel pots are in front of her and she quietly fills the styrofoam cups with corn, then meat, then fruit, and water and hands them into the circle.

Grover is speaking now, in Cheyenne, and from John's response, there is sufficient praise for his architectural contribution to tradition. Others follow, each is eloquent and without religious fervor or pretense. Each tells of his or her medicine dreams during the night or merely expresses gratitude to John for putting up the meeting. Some offer personal experiences of how peyote and the

Native Church have helped them. Each affirms his or her faith, which is as obvious to all as the ground we sit on.

And now it is silent. John is looking at me. He has introduced me as a friend of Tom's. I know I'm expected to speak, but I'm faltering. I feel some words come out—a thank you—and then nothing. I'm suddenly deaf to my own words. I feel my voice working, but I don't know what I'm saying. I want to tell him about my dream and the Métis children that I grew up with on the west side of Great Falls. I want to tell everyone about Robert Falcon and Jim and me and how I'd not thought about them until this night, with the help of the medicine. And then as suddenly as it appeared, the dream is coming out of my mouth and I'm telling it all. And then it stops, and I falter into another awkward silence. John intervenes. His voice is soft, in the distance, as he speaks.

> Cheyenne people like to pray a long time. Once we had a prayer meeting on the Ashland Divide, in the old way, in a tipi. There was an Arapaho man there, and in the morning he wanted to pray and make his prayer a good long one. He prayed for each person in the tipi and their families; he called each one by name. Then he prayed for everyone in his family and named them all too. He prayed for the president of the United States and Congress and the Supreme Court. He prayed for all the Cheyenne people and the Arapaho people and named as many as he could. He prayed for all the white people in the world and named the ones he knew. He prayed for all the animals and everything in nature. After a pretty long time he was running out of things to pray for. Then an airplane flew over the tipi, and so he prayed for the pilot and the crew and all the passengers. Then he was stuck. He looked down at the ground. Right in front of him there was a big hill of red ants. He looked very relieved and pointed at the hill and said, "And, Heavenly Father, we even pray for these ants!" Just then, one bit him right on his fingertip. He jumped a little and said, "We pray they don't bite us so hard!" It was a good prayer.

The water tastes sweet beneath John's closing prayer. Around the circle, most have put sunglasses on; the sunlight is a little oppres-

sive for dilated pupils. And now we rise and file out into the morning air. We all shake hands and say "good morning." There will be
a feast later, but Tom and I must excuse ourselves. We have a long
drive ahead of us, and the weather is good. I look at John and I'm
speechless once again. We shake hands and say "good morning."

Irene looked less tearful and finally smiled when I finished telling
about my first peyote meeting. As promised, Tom and I had
stopped by on our way out of town on the morning after. Henry was
busy on the front porch butchering his night's work—a very large
whitetail buck. Irene was deeply pleased by my favorable review of
peyote and the meeting.

   Now, Irene and I were quiet again, and I was remembering how,
once we got back to Missoula, I had drafted letter after letter to
John Woodenlegs, each one failing to convey my deep response to
the meeting and my respect for him and all those present. Eventually I sent one of those letters, after I had given in to the impossi-
bility of the task. Remembering it now, I can say that if I have had a
religious experience in my life, it was at that meeting. I said something like that to him in the letter.

   On that last day, when I sat with Irene Tall Bull, I was reminded
of a word from classical Greek: *kenosis*. It means vain, hollow, fruit-
less, void—empty. Early Christian theology used the term to mark
the process through which Christ emptied himself of his divinity
so that he could enter the human world and be crucified. Certainly,
in most of the world's religions, emptiness or the "emptying out"
of the psyche is the prerequisite for sacramental experience. Although deeply uncertain about it all on that morning, there in the
half-light and silence of her living room I sat with Irene Tall Bull
and thought about peyote and Henry and *kenosis*.

3

The Polaroids were still on her lap. All the while I had talked about the peyote meeting, her hands had circled them, her fingertips just touching the corners. I looked at my own hands folded in my lap and turned my wrist slightly to look at my watch. Then I recoiled; I was embarrassed by the reflex and hoped she didn't see. And I was surprised by the time distortion. We had relived so much in less than an hour.

But it was still June 1976, and much time had passed since my first peyote meeting—almost four years. I attended several meetings after that first one, each more enlightening than the last.

I looked at Irene and realized it was only the second time we had been alone together. I tried to catalogue mentally the number of my visits since that first night, but already the dates and events were starting to merge and fade. I had made perhaps two dozen visits over a period of eighteen months, maybe fewer, and most of those were brief, lasting no more than a few days. After that, maybe half a dozen, spread over two more years. The brevity of it all seemed incredible—too few days for all that had happened. I felt a twinge of panic. I wanted to keep all the memories, but I knew I was going to forget many things, perhaps too much. Once I left her house that morning, I didn't think I would ever see Irene Tall Bull again, and I didn't want to forget, because she, more than anyone I'd met, had demonstrated the way to live the good life.

Irene Tall Bull knew that life's goodness was determined by a sense of humor. It was humor that saved us from adversity, and to laugh in its face was her first line of defense. She fiercely refused to be driven into despair by the antics of a world she judged as fundamentally absurd and therefore hilarious on a cosmic scale.

The absurdity she perceived was cross-cultural, interracial, ecumenical, and centered on the delusion that humans can control the world—specifically the behaviors of other humans, and generally the environment at large. Irene knew that this delusion invariably leads to blunder and catastrophe, and so most absurd of all were, of course, those claiming immunity from the ravages of human blunderings. But the most delusional of all human endeavors, by her definition, were those exercised in the name of the common good. And so Irene Tall Bull was ever on the alert to detect and make public any and every appearance of human nonsense.

She took great delight in the monthly arrival of her one and only allotment check, her share of a piece of tribal land sold to the government under the policies of the "Dead Indian Act" of 1902. As an extension of the Dawes Act of 1887, which placed unallotted Indian land "in trust," the Dead Indian Act enabled white ranchers who were pressuring the government for more range land to acquire it for nothing. When the original allottees died, their land could be sold to the government and the proceeds divided among their heirs. The land was then offered within land grant statutes to white ranchers. When the Indian Reorganization Act of 1934 came into effect, however, the Cheyennes could begin reclaiming much of what had been sold, and many Cheyenne families received federal payments for land lost under the Dead Indian Act. The monthly payments were divided equally among the members of each family. Irene's family was among these, but the number of heirs had increased greatly since 1902.

Nevertheless, the government honored its contract and sent her a U.S. Treasury Department check for four cents every single month. Upon its arrival she would remove its predecessor from the kitchen wall and replace it with the new check, noting with glee that the stamp on the envelope had more cash value than her land. She never cashed any of the checks, hoping she had released a bookkeeping virus into the federal treasury. But the checks kept coming anyway, and without comment, which only confirmed a deeper truth about federal Indian policy. As Irene said each time she tacked the new check on the wall, "There—now I'm a good dead Indian!"

But it was commodities day at Lame Deer Agency that received top billing in her reservation theater of the absurd, and she never failed to send Henry into town to pick up their share. This was welfare roulette BIA style, and everybody was a winner.

Each family got a package labeled in military stencils: "U.S. Government Surplus Commodities." The actual contents, however, were selected through a mysterious bureaucratic process lacking any purpose beyond an attempt at complete random distribution of loosely related articles. Recipients would be blessed with a carton of Similac (usually when they had no babies), or perhaps Korean War K rations. Sometimes there was an assortment of canned fruit and vegetables plus several cans whose labels had been lost shortly after V-J Day. Irene assumed that these contained beans, but she never had the courage to open one.

The surprises were always accompanied by a pair of two-pound bricks of processed yellow cheese, reminiscent of Velveeta but more viscous and tasteless. And as proof of governmental concern for public welfare and the Quartermaster Corps's assault on entropy, the cheese was always accompanied by twelve-ounce bags of lentils and macaroni—one of each. Once, Irene offered the cheese to me, but when she considered the possibility that my children might eat it and thereby suffer permanently impacted bowels, she promptly withdrew the gift.

Occasionally, the melange was graced with five pounds of ground meat, frozen and unspecified as to species. The label, "U.S. Government Issue—Ground Meat," implied that it was hamburger; however, in remembrance of government conspiracies historically, Irene assumed that it was horse meat. Nonetheless, like a child on Christmas morning she would gleefully open the box and squeal, "Oh Henry, look what we got! I wonder what I should cook for dinner!" She would hold up two cans without labels and grin. "Isn't the BIA good to us!?"

But after the box could generate no more laughter, Henry took the commodities away to a house where they indeed represented relief. And somehow, the carton always magically acquired a few pounds of fresh venison in transit.

As a counterweight to Irene's intellectual taste for the absurd, Henry offered real skills to enact all manner of rebellion. It was a balance that both recognized from the beginning of their marriage, each appreciative of the capabilities of the other. For where Irene could only dream, Henry could produce real revolution and was, in the tradition of Cheyenne warriors, utterly fearless. Together, they were minimally mischievous, potentially dangerous.

But when it came to acquiring fresh meat, they were the Bonnie and Clyde of the Northern Cheyenne reservation.

Henry's survival skills had been acquired through necessity. He was born into that time in reservation history where commodities day meant pretty much what it meant in 1971—short rations. To survive, Cheyenne families needed to be resourceful. So, without any reasonable assurance of steady employment on the reservation, they grew gardens, practiced traditional gathering ways, and hunted.

When he was twelve years old, Henry received a 22-caliber rifle and a box of shells from his father. The gift was at once a reward celebrating his natural talent as a sharpshooter and a marker announcing his passage into manhood. From that day forward it was Henry's responsibility to keep the family supplied with meat for the winter, and he had to accomplish the task with that single box of shells. Fifty shots were all his father could afford to buy.

Although those times were hard, Henry was proud when he told about them. He said he was terrified that first winter, for he missed many shots and was sure the bullets would not last and his family would go hungry. But then he found his stride and killed two enormous bucks to make up for the loss of ammunition. He rarely missed after that.

Once they were married, it was a matter of course that Irene would become Henry's hunting partner, especially when she learned that they were, for the most part, poaching. When hunting deer off the reservation and out of season, Henry taught her that night time was the right time. To his great delight, her night vision was on a par with his marksmanship, and so on moonless, occluded nights they drove the darkened car across the plains to stalk the elusive whitetail.

The strategy was simple. Henry drove with the lights off while Irene scanned the darkness for telltale shape and movement. The deer, also taking advantage of the starless night, were bolder, often browsing in clearings or at the edge of the woods where they were vulnerable—unfortunately so when Irene and Henry were hunting, because if Irene saw them first, there was no contest.

Fortunately for the whitetail, however, no matter how skillful the stalker, the balance favors the prey. After one particularly dark night, Henry and Irene found themselves driving into the sunrise along a lonely dirt road far from the reservation. They'd not seen a deer all night.

A rancher's fence ran parallel to the road, and beyond it, bunches of yearling calves huddled against the morning chill. Irene looked longingly at those plump cattle and began to muse out loud about how tender and sweet they would taste; again and again she pointed to one and then another until she was positively salivating with desire.

Suddenly, Henry stopped the car, looked at her tenderly, and asked, "Which one would you like?" She praised them all again, and the rancher for keeping them well, and then pointed to one near the fence. Without further comment, Henry aimed the rifle through the open window and dropped the calf where it stood. Irene registered her protest and disbelief with an ultrasonic squeal and hand-wringing while Henry got out, dragged the calf under the fence, and quickly stowed it in the trunk. It was all over in seconds, but it was several minutes down the road before Irene's squeal had descended into a mantra: "Oooh Henry!! I didn't really mean you should shoot it! Oooh Henry! . . . "

When they told the story to Tom and me, it was evident that the calf had tasted all the sweeter for the circumstances of its demise. Henry said, "When I got back in the car I told Irene, I only aim to please you." After a nostalgic giggle, Irene said, "It tasted good, but we gave most of it to Belle Highwalking. When Henry went to visit her, all she had to eat was chokecherry gravy."

Henry smiled and looked at me thoughtfully. I knew what he was thinking even before he asked if I liked to hunt. So I wasn't surprised when he disappeared into the back bedroom one evening and returned with his rifle. It was a 22-caliber bolt-action single shot with a long barrel—the one his father had given him when he was twelve. He removed the bolt and checked the barrel and then said to Irene, "Let's go hunting." Tom and I looked at each other and knew that we were wondering what the prey of choice would be that night.

There was little time for reflection. In seconds, Irene's stiff arthritic legs had quickstepped her body out of the house, leaving Tom and me standing in the dark. With Henry already warming up the car, whatever moral ambiguity we still harbored about poaching had to be compromised. We shut the door quickly behind us.

It was a starless late winter night on the cusp of the Ides of March, with warm air and cold air undulating around and through each other. Henry headed the car south toward Birney village but soon turned off the road and cut the headlights. Several minutes passed before I could see him and Irene in the front seat or Tom next to me or even my hands held close to my face. The car seemed to float. No one spoke and we all kept our breathing below a whisper.

At last the landscape emerged and drifted past the car like an abstract expressionist painting, each shape melting into the next until all sensations of the car dissolved. Inside the shadow dream, while the car seemed to direct its own course along the endless horizon, I saw all manner of beasts, ghouls, and people but no deer.

It was well after midnight when Irene's sharp whisper broke the silence: "Henry! Stop the car!" With a sideways movement of her lips and a quick jerk of her head she indicated a location on her side of the car. "Do you see them? Over there by that bush—a buck and a doe!" He followed her gesture into the void. "I see them."

He was out of the car in an instant and hunched over the hood with the rifle aimed into the blackness. Tom and I squinted through the window and then slid out of the car hoping to see the deer—or even the bush—but we were barely upright when the rifle popped. Then silence, followed quickly by a dull thud and Irene's whisper: "Do you see the doe, Henry? She's behind the bush!" Then another "pop," then silence, and a softer fall.

Henry leaned the rifle against the wheel well and moved slowly around the car. Tom and I followed. The doe and buck, each with a bullet in its brain, were dead before they hit the ground. Both held a look of surprise in their eyes even as their bodies grew cold. Irene had the trunk open and lined with a tarp by the time we got the carcasses back to the car. Our exit was quick and silent.

We restrained ourselves all the way home. Even the headlights remained off until we were within a mile of Lame Deer. Only when they were safe at last inside the kitchen did the hunters' howling and laughter explode into the muted dawn. Only then did the hunters boast of and retell and magnify the exploits of the night while they feasted on deer liver and tasted the primal flavor of the hunt. Only then, amid the afterglow and the sunlight, was I privileged to see Henry Tall Bull for the first time—the Henry Tall Bull who was a man, fierce, proud, and compassionate. Only then was

I privileged to see him in the absence of that other Henry Tall Bull, the one I'd touched briefly beneath the scars on his forehead.

My talk about our hunting adventures had at last brought a smile.

"We had good times then," Irene said. "A lot of old people got fed with those deer."

I nodded and looked down. Somehow I'd held on to one of the Polaroids. I looked at Henry's face and my hand shook as I handed the picture back to her. I recovered and asked if she remembered when Tom and I brought our families to Lame Deer for a powwow. She nodded and blinked back her tears.

"We had a good time at the Ice Well," she said.

It was hot that weekend, and I had driven all night from Missoula and followed the full moon across the Gallatin valley while my family slept. Then, as the car climbed the rimrocks outside of Billings, the sun rose as the moon set, and we were caught in the cross-light of their immensity.

I had hoped for a few cool hours of sleep when we got to the powwow grounds, but it was already 85 degrees when I began setting up our old army tent next to a Southern Cheyenne family. They had done this before: their four-posted white canvas house tent, fully equipped with cots, comfortable chairs, and a potbelly stove, clearly outclassed ours. The white canvas kept the tent cool inside, and they sat beneath the awning in front and watched me sweat. Soon all the neighboring children came to watch. Taking great delight in catching the enormous grasshoppers, they were ecstatic to discover my wife's bug phobia and sent her screaming when they held the glistening, wiggling bodies close to her face. I felt the heat rising and wished we'd accepted Irene's invitation to stay with her.

When at last the tent was up, my Cheyenne neighbor shared his water with me, and we talked about our children and powwows and my wife's fear of insects. And then I found my bedroll and the cooler dark of the tent and slept until the heat drove me from it.

There was a standpipe about fifty yards from the tent and the line of people to it was longer than that. Each filled a bucket, dumped its contents over his head and then filled it again for the campsite. Someone had hung a thermometer on the post behind the pipe—118 degrees, and it was just 1:00 P.M. I doused myself twice and was halfway back to the tent when Henry appeared.

"I got some ribs. Irene wants to go up to the Ice Well for a barbecue. Maybe you'd bring your family. It's too hot down here. You can come back tonight for the dancing."

The Ice Well was a glacial phenomenon that gave the Ashland Divide some of the glamour of Yellowstone Park. Near the summit of the divide the earth housed a large area of perennial ice about fifteen feet below its surface. This subterranean remnant of the Ice Age seemed even more improbable than geysers or mud pots. Henry said people used to harvest the ice, but now it was just a curiosity and a place to cool off on hot summer days.

Soon we were relaxing in the pines on the Ashland Divide and taking turns climbing down the well into nature's refrigerator, marveling at the extruded block of ice and our own gooseflesh in the midst of summer as we held our bare feet against it. And while our barbecue simmered, Henry took the children on a nature walk and showed them a dozen or more medicinal and edible plants.

He chuckled while they chewed the small tubers he'd produced from the seemingly barren soil at the base of a pine tree, and I saw the spark of awakening in my son's eyes as he took it all in—making the connection between earth and subsistence for the first time. Henry saw it too and said, "When I was scoutmaster, we went on camping trips and only ate what we could catch and gather." My daughter looked at him incredulously, while the boys ran off in search of more edibles, which they brought to Henry for approval, asking again and again, "Can you eat this?" until their foraging disintegrated and they brought pebbles and sticks and he called off the expedition. They hung on his hands and arms as they all came to the fire for ribs and corn on the cob.

I was sure I heard her laugh when I talked about Henry and the kids at the Ice Well, and so I started to babble, trying to retrieve any and every memory of the good times, to build a buffer against amnesia. I reminded her of our feast at the Ice Well that day, and how Henry wouldn't eat because we'd forgotten the salt and he couldn't eat the meat and corn without it. Since I couldn't bear to see him go hungry, I said I had to have salt too and then got in the car and drove the twelve miles to the powwow ground to fetch some. I thought she might laugh again when I told her about the commodities I found stacked neatly on the picnic table at my tent; members of the tribal council had given a BIA "care" package to every camper.

Mine had been cooking all afternoon in the 120-degree heat. The "ground meat" had thawed and was at the edge of spoiling. I thought she might joke about the rations, but I was wrong. Her lip quivered and the tears spread quickly over her cheeks.

I gave her my handkerchief and watched her grief rise—not from the singular fact of death but from the minutiae of life, the ordinary particulars, unique to each person, that somehow define a life. "I told him he used too much salt but he always wanted more!"

Seeing her grief was harder than expressing my own. I pushed it down and watched until she caught her breath and dabbed at her cheeks with the handkerchief. And then I reminded her that this was only the second time we'd been alone together and that this was the only time I'd come to Lame Deer just to visit her. She looked a little puzzled until I asked if she thought the neighbors would talk. And then she did smile and chuckled a little. "Alex came back after you left that first time. He wanted to know what you ate."

I reached into the bag I'd carried from the car and withdrew a typescript with Belle Highwalking's portrait as the cover. I handed the book to Irene. "I thought you might like to see this. It's her life story, the one she recorded in Missoula with Tobie. Helen Highwalker made the translation, and the Council for Indian Education is going to publish it. There are more portraits inside."

She blinked once more and put the Polaroids back on her lap and looked at Belle's quiet face hovering in the shadows. "It's a good picture. She was so good to everyone. Her grandchildren will love this book when they get older. All the pictures are good, Jerry." And then she looked at the words—I wasn't sure if she read or just looked at the words, Belle's words—as the collected remainders of a life.

Her story contained nothing remarkable. Belle had lived through times with elders whose history had been indeed momentous, but her own life had been the day-to-day life of a traditional Cheyenne woman, and most of that lived within the locale of Lame Deer. When she met Tobie and learned a little about anthropology and cultural preservation, she wanted to contribute, as many other elders had done. Her brother, John Stands In Timber, had in a way prepared the ground for her with his narrative, "Cheyenne Memories," done with Margot Liberty. When she told Tobie she wanted to record her story and Tobie agreed to help her, Belle's visits to

Missoula became more frequent and longer. They sat night after night in Tobie's kitchen while Belle spoke softly into the tape recorder. About a year after she finished the recording, Belle died.

I told Irene I had special affection for Belle. She had been, after all, the tipping point that began all my journeys to Lame Deer. And during those first few months she and Grover were the only Cheyenne elders I visited. Her cabin, one of the last of its type in Lame Deer, was always snug, especially in winter. I remembered that February day when Tom and I visited and she at last relaxed around me and giggled because I wanted to take her picture again. That day I stepped outside for a cigarette amid a light snowfall and was surprised by Belle's granddaughter, who suddenly peeked out the door at me and laughed, and I returned the favor by snapping her picture: a round, curious face within the weathered door frame, her black eyes narrowed against the snowflakes, her form dwarfed by century-old logs—just the face beneath the icicles.

When summer came I made another photograph of a child at Belle's cabin, one of Myrna's friends, leaning against the cabin wall, holding a large ball, waiting to play. Whatever the season, when Belle was at home, Lame Deer children were at her cabin—she was their grandmother.

Belle could have lived anywhere she chose in Lame Deer, especially after the 1963 claims settlement. But she preferred her cabin, even with its lack of plumbing, limited electrical service, and rough wood floor only recently elevated from the dirt. Like most folks in Lame Deer, she had no telephone, but her cabin had a new tin roof. It was the home she'd moved into after her husband, Floyd, died, and it was like the log home they'd shared throughout more than fifty years of marriage. They met when she was sixteen, and she was proud of their mutual faithfulness: "He never even looked at another woman," she said, "and I had no time for other men."

Belle could have had a new pre-fab like Henry and Irene, but the cabin reminded her of Floyd and life on the reservation between the world wars—the times she and other Cheyenne elders called the "good old days." Those days, which filled the bulk of her narrative, had indeed been good for her and Floyd, as well as most other Cheyenne families at that time. Even though government services and programs were scant, the Cheyennes, retaining their sense of community and their familial values, shared and "made do" within limited resources.

Belle and Floyd lived their lives and made their living the way everyone did on the reservation then—by gardening, raising some stock, taking odd jobs, and supplementing these with government rations. It is true that their reservation was the poorest of the seven in Montana, but they did not starve. More important, they retained the old ways of living together as Cheyennes.

Like most Cheyennes, Belle was a deeply religious person. And, like many, she found no contradiction in the observance of both traditional Cheyenne ceremonies and Christian church services. She talked about that in her narrative.

"My husband and I were peyote people. When we were young, we liked this way. Whenever we heard about a peyote meeting, we just had to go. My oldest son was small then. We used to go with Black Wolf, who was a highly respected man in the peyote way. His wife and I stayed together during the meetings. We also went with Ernest King and his wife when she was alive. When we had peyote meetings, we put up a tipi and prayed all night. Many times we did this, and once we put up two tipis. Everything was plentiful then; we had cattle and butchered a beef because everyone likes meat. We used to go in a wagon to Kirby or Busby or Ashland, and big crowds came to the meetings.

"When my son Max was sick, we put up peyote meetings to help him get well. We did this several times. We prayed for him, but he died anyway. I still kept on going after that, but I couldn't stop thinking about my son every time I went in the tipi. I started to get ill thinking about him, and that's when I stopped going. I don't go anymore, but my son George still goes.

"The Catholic priests were here a long time, and I went there when I first got married. My children and my husband were baptized in that church. We did everything they told us to do. On Fridays and Wednesdays we didn't eat meat. We went to confession on Christmas and also on egg-dying day. Then after we had gone a long time, something came up, and people tattled to the priest that we went to peyote meetings. They told mostly about me, because my husband hadn't joined yet. When I went to confession, the priest questioned me. He asked, "I heard that you go to peyote meetings and go around with peyote people. Is that so? You pray to a dried-up peyote and you have him for your God." This is what he told me. I said, "No. I don't pray to that dried thing. I pray to God, and I use peyote for medicine. Sometimes I get sick and use it.

Then I get well." This is what I told him. He said, "You call it a church. No one can go to two places at one time. You must just come here or go to the peyote church."

"I felt hurt, but I never told him anything. I didn't say I wouldn't come back or anything. I just felt bad because I had just lost my child, my youngest girl. I prayed for her, but in spite of this, she died. These two things made me quit going to the Catholic Church. I used to work for the church for a long time, never drawing wages but donating my services. The older priests asked me to come back, but I didn't do it. The one who said those things to me was not a good priest and said bad things.

"I go to the Mennonite Church now and I like this way. They read and speak in Cheyenne, and this is where I began to learn to read the Bible in Cheyenne. I never understood or spoke English too well, but now I am learning to read Cheyenne. I am included in their committees and am able to help out even though I'm old."

Belle's happiest recollections were those of the days and weeks she and Floyd spent on trips to Oklahoma to visit relatives. They made those trips in a horse-drawn wagon and camped along the way. As was the custom, their visits lasted many days, and relatives often returned with them to Lame Deer. Indeed, in the good-weather months, visitation between Northern and Southern Cheyennes was constant. Belle expressed distress over the arrival of the automobile on the reservation: "When people got cars, they stopped visiting."

As Irene and I talked about Belle, I realized how easy it is to forget that the Cheyennes love the Tongue River country and wanted to have their reservation here. Like Belle, who kept her cabin because it reminded her of happy times with Floyd and her young family, the Cheyennes loved the Tongue River country because it was the place where they had thrived as a nation, and they believed they could continue nowhere else. In the end, their isolation on the reserve, for all its deleterious effects, enabled them to preserve their way, the Cheyenne way. And that way is to live a life simply for the sake of living it within what they call the natural order.

Visitation is at the core of the Cheyenne way. It binds and affirms all the spiritual and practical elements of the society. Visiting relatives and friends affirms all kinship relationships, beginning with respect for elders. And all ceremonial practice flows from these, because the life of the people and their continued existence depends upon the continuum of relationships from the Heavenly Father down to the inert center of the earth—the natural order.

Belle and Floyd did not, of course, speak of it as philosophy; they lived it. It was only when the continuum of connections began to rupture with the intrusion of white technology that Belle noticed the change and felt its consequence—loneliness. Nonetheless, she held to the old way, so it was only natural that on one of her visits to Missoula to speak her story into the tape recorder, she was compelled by the Cheyenne way to ask Tobie if she could come across the street to my house to visit—not me, but my mother.

My mother was astonished and uncertain as to why this woman whom she did not know wanted to visit her. Yet she too was compelled by a tradition of courtesy, and in a flurry she brewed fresh coffee, readied the teapot, and arranged a plate of her homemade bread, cookies, jam, and cake. Soon enough, Belle emerged from Tom's front porch with her perennial shawl wrapped tightly around her cheeks and made her way across the street, walking with tiny, prancing steps.

She knocked, my mother answered, and she entered. I made the formal introductions and retired to the next room, where I feigned work at my stand-up writing desk. Belle sat perched on the edge of her chair, knees together, hands folded in her lap. My mother, visibly awkward and uncertain, did the same until, after a silence exceedingly long for her, she offered Belle refreshments. And then it was my turn to be astonished.

Here were two women, elders in their respective communities, who had lived their lives concurrently at opposite ends of the Montana high plains, representing cultural polarities formed within a history neither of them understood. My mother had lived her life in a state containing seven Indian reservations without ever having had tea with a Native American in any context, let alone her own home. Nor had she ever visited any of those reservations. Belle, who had grown up fearful of white people, especially white men, only through her recent and deep attachment to Tobie had begun to extend herself beyond the perceptual boundaries of Lame Deer. Yet here they were, facing each other over tea and cake, groping for common ground between sips and nibbles.

But my musing on historical irony and sychronicity soon faded when they at last found something they could share with complete agreement and understanding: the utter wickedness of their sons. And with that they entered the portals of the universal coffee klatch, which transcends all cultural barriers—that insular place where the unvarnished truth about men as only women can know it may be revealed. And they revealed it with great delight for the better part of an hour.

Within the course of that hour, wherein I clearly needed to maintain the lowest of profiles, there was a moment when my mother cast a glance at me over her shoulder, and I caught it. It was the look of one who had been completely disarmed, and I was certain in that instant that she suddenly understood why Belle had come to visit.

My mother was an elder and so it was required, since Belle knew me, for her to be respectful and visit my mother. And, by extension, respect was offered to me and my wife and children. My mother had never been so simply honored before, and she was deeply moved. And, as that quick glance over her shoulder had so precisely communicated, Belle's gesture had been made despite the vagaries and indecencies of history, despite the humiliation of poverty.

Irene listened to me and thumbed through the printed narrative, pausing for a long time at each picture. She smiled when I noted that while she worked on it with Tobie, Belle visited my mother often, and it was during those visits that I made the best photographs of her, the ones in the book.

There was an easy silence after Irene closed the cover and placed Belle's narrative on her lap, on top of the Polaroids of Henry. I thought about Belle and how fitting it was that this gentle, modest woman who had unwittingly precipitated my involvement with her people would, in the end, spend a few of her last days in my home. Over coffee and the ordinary talk among friends she had demonstrated the natural order that puts the world before life, life before humans, and the respect of others before the love of self.

4

Henry Tall Bull was dead. Within that unspoken fact and the shaded light of her living room, Irene and I sat and faced each other. His death surrounded us, but we did not speak his name. Cheyennes don't mention the names of their dead relatives because nothing should be done that might impede their journey to the spirit world. Spoken names might confuse the departed or tempt them to return to this world to haunt it.

Even though we hadn't said his name, I felt haunted by Henry. I wanted to say something about all the good work he had done for the writing project. I worried that the stigma of his drinking might have diminished the value of his contribution in the minds of some tribal members, and I wanted to defend him in case Irene had felt the brunt of criticism. But she spoke first.

"Tom came to the funeral. There were lots of people who came. Tom was good to us. He worked so hard on the children's books. He was glad Tom was here to help with that project."

And then it was my turn to feel the tears rise, and my body shuddered beneath them. I swallowed hard and then apologized for not coming to the funeral—but I couldn't tell her that I just had not been able to force myself, even when Tom invited me to come with him. And the dread I had felt then rose again as I looked at Irene, still unable to sort out my conflict or even begin to express my sense of failure. She saw me struggling and spoke again.

"John Woodenlegs was at the funeral and he said a lot of good things. He came and visited me afterward too—he offered to be Road Chief for a peyote meeting if I wanted to put it up. He was very kind."

I nodded and felt my tears escape. I fought against them but she saw them anyway.

"Oooh Jerry!—It's all right. We thought about you. John Woodenlegs said you helped us a lot with the Marquis pictures. We knew you couldn't make it to the funeral—Tom said you had to work."

She got up and went to the kitchen for more coffee. "They always had fun at the meetings." She spoke from the kitchen and her voice was suddenly comforting, confident, the way I'd always known it. "They told so many stories they hardly got any work done!"

We both laughed. "I remember," I said. "The first time I met with the cultural association, we were supposed to talk about the Marquis photographs but spent most of the time talking about collecting stories. I remember Tom kept trying to change the subject, but it was no use."

She brought the coffeepot with her and poured while I talked about that first meeting.

Tom and I had made an extra trip to Lame Deer that month. The cultural association wanted to know how he was doing with the Cheyenne history he was preparing for use in the schools. Tom thought there might be a chance to talk about the collection of photographs that John Woodenlegs had recently acquired. They were made on the reservation by a doctor, Thomas B. Marquis, in the 1920s and '30s. His daughters had given the shoebox full of negatives to John, who didn't know what to do with them, so he gave them to Tom. We didn't know much about Marquis then. He had been the agency physician in the 1920s, and later he devoted his time to Cheyenne history and became a self-taught ethnographer.

"I'll never forget the night Tom came over to my house with the Marquis collection," I said.

Irene sipped and nodded. She liked this story. It had all the mystery of archaeological discovery and the wonder of salvaged treasure.

Tom had appeared on my doorstep, breathless, holding the box in both hands. John Woodenlegs had been in town for a visit, and when Tom took him to the airport, John handed him the shoebox and said, "Would you do something with this for me? Marquis's daughters gave it to me. They said the tribe should have it, but I don't know what to do with old picture negatives."

We sat on the couch in my living room and Tom showed me the prize.

The box was jammed with hundreds of negatives and a few small prints, all of them dusty, loose, and unprotected. The emulsion on several had started to slough off, and some were on the edge of disintegration. The obvious next step was to head for my darkroom. In minutes, we got our first look at reservation life in the 1920s.

The first print showed a group of men loading sacks onto a horse-drawn wagon in front of the old Lame Deer flour mill. Next was a view of an open field with many Cheyennes working together, cutting up meat on ration day. I printed several more, each a remarkably candid view of daily life during an important time on the reservation. Most of the elders alive at that time had known the Cheyenne way of life before there had been reservations, and several of the men had participated in the Custer fight.

Tom and I were overwhelmed. A rough count revealed close to five hundred negatives in the box. Few, if any, had ever been published, and Tom doubted if many Cheyennes had seen them. We spent the next several days considering how much work it would take to restore the collection. Tom wanted me to do the work, and we planned a restoration proposal for the upcoming meeting of the association.

The road to Lame Deer seemed extra long that weekend. The meeting was scheduled for Saturday morning at nine. Tom, Henry, and I were fashionably late at nine-thirty. No one else was there. John Woodenlegs showed up a little after ten, and over the next forty-five minutes most of the committee arrived. I waited expectantly, Marquis prints in hand, but there was no apparent agenda, and soon we were all drifting from one story to the next.

After half an hour or so, John looked at me and said, "You did pretty good with that gourd at the prayer meeting." I was appropriately modest. "Thank you for the letter," he continued, "it was a good letter."

I took this as an invitation to speak and reached for my envelope full of prints. But before I could start, John had gone another way.

"Our history is very important to us," he began. "The stories that our grandparents told us about the old ways—these are the ones that tell us how to live. If we don't keep these stories, the Cheyenne way will disappear." Everyone made sounds of approval.

There was an interval of silence. I looked at Tom for guidance. He shrugged and waited.

"Tom Weist and Henry Tall Bull have been collecting stories for us," John continued, and although he didn't look at me, I knew he was talking to me. "Henry goes out and meets with our old folks and he records their stories. We have a good field tape recorder. Then he and Tom put them in writing. They've been gathering children's stories for the bilingual program. We're going to publish them in English and Cheyenne. They've already got several books done. It's a wonderful project."

Again, general approval was voiced by the group, followed by another silence. This time I waited. John Woodenlegs was speaking for my benefit, to let me know the value of what the association was trying to accomplish. Also, as a medicine man and a chief, he was following tradition by setting the context for the meeting and extending his courtesy to me.

"The elders tell the stories to their grandchildren so they will learn what it means to be Cheyenne. Most of all, Cheyennes are brave, courageous people. Our soldiers have always been brave. Being brave is the most important. After that, the stories teach our children to help and respect their families, and we do that by sharing everything. Cheyennes are not stingy or selfish. Even if we have nothing, we share a glass of water."

I listened and remembered my first peyote meeting. I remembered John Woodenlegs wrapping the peyote robe around the shoulders of the young man who prayed for his lost father. I remembered the profound tenderness John exhibited as he prayed with that young man. After that meeting I learned from Tom that John had lost a son to alcoholism and suicide. John never spoke about his son, but that tragedy had only strengthened his belief that the peyote way and the current cultural renaissance could save Cheyenne culture and provide health for their young people.

He looked at me and said, "Now we have the bilingual program, and our children can learn to read the Cheyenne language, and they can read about their history."

And then, after a longer silence, "Cheyennes believe in the natural order. That means that everything, from earth to sky, is alive, even stones and air. We believe everything has its place, and when everything is in its place there is peace. That's the natural order. That's what the stories teach. Many of our young people are forgetting these ways. That's why we need the writing project and the bilingual program. So they won't forget."

He paused again. This time he did want a response from me, and when I praised their work, he beamed. "Tom and Henry have shown me their books and told me some of the new stories they're working on. I especially like the 'Popping Machine' story."

John laughed. "Oh yeah. The one where grandfather gets a new Model T in Forsythe and takes off driving without any lessons. He thinks it's like a horse and you have to break it so it will obey. His grandson is with him, but he can't drive either. And then, just when they realize they don't have brakes, the instruction book blows away and they can't stop. When they get back to Lame Deer, they still can't stop and the grandson jumps off the car, but grandfather keeps on driving. Finally, he just turns the wheel and lets the car go in a big circle all around the house—all night long until he runs out of gas! That's a good one!"

When the laughter died down, John asked Henry if he'd gotten any stories from Willis Medicine Bull.

"I've been to see him, but he hasn't told any stories yet. I think he's a little shy about talking into the tape recorder."

Tom started to chuckle: "I love that story about Willis's dad and the stool specimen."

"Oh yeah," Henry said, "that was when there was a cholera epidemic on the reservation before World War I. The public health doctor had to check everybody on the reservation, and the way they did it was to get a stool specimen from each person." John was already laughing but Henry went on.

"Willis's father didn't speak English, and so the white doctor had to have an interpreter tell the old man what he wanted. The interpreter was a young Cheyenne man, and he was really nervous because Willis's dad was an Old Man Chief. But he was nervous mostly because there's no word in Cheyenne for 'stool specimen.' He talked all around it for quite a while and finally the old man got mad and scolded him and said, 'Just tell me what the white man wants!' The boy gave up and said, very softly, 'The white doctor wants your shit.'

"Then the old man got really mad and yelled, 'God damn white man! First he killed all the buffalo, then he took our land, took our horses—now he wants our shit!' "

The room exploded. John shielded his mouth with his hand but was belly-laughing hard. And as the laughter eased, more stories came, one after another for the better part of an hour. Yet all the while, the business of the association was conducted. Within the weave of story and laughter, papers were signed, projects updated, paychecks issued. I forgot all about the Marquis photographs until I realized that the meeting was winding down, and a few people were excusing themselves. At last, Tom intervened.

"John, I had a chance to look at the Marquis collection, and Jerry made a few prints. It's pretty impressive."

I handed the envelope to John, and the few who were about to leave returned to their seats.

On top of the stack was a photograph of an elder sitting in profile on his horse near a grandstand. He's wearing a cowboy hat and sunglasses and appears to be watching something.

John was excited. "This is Iron Shirt. He was a famous man—fought Custer. He's at Crow fairgrounds in this picture. That's the grandstand. I think he's watching the horse races. When the reservation was first started, he got into trouble with some white cattlemen.

"There were these homesteaders, Zook and Alderson. They had a place near the old Lame Deer Agency. One day, one of their hands bet another one he could shoot the hat off a sleeping Cheyenne without hurting him. The one they had in mind was Black Wolf. He was a chief. But the cowboy didn't aim so good, and Black Wolf got knocked out when the bullet grazed his head. When he came to, everybody was gone, and so he walked three miles to his camp and told his relatives. I guess the two cowboys went for help, but when they came back, Black Wolf's people were waiting. They shot the cowboys and burned the house down."

"I heard that a posse from Miles City came and arrested thirteen Cheyennes for the incident," Tom said. "Four of them got five years in prison for burning the house, but Black Wolf and the rest were acquitted."

"Yeah," said John. "After that, Zook and Alderson got a new homestead in the Tongue River country by Hanging Woman Creek. Iron Shirt's place was nearby, and I guess another one of Alderson's men ran some cattle right through Iron Shirt's garden. They got into an argument about it, and the cowboy shot Iron Shirt. The bullet broke his arm. But the cowboy turned himself in and he got off scot-free. This is a good picture."

And so it went for another hour. Each picture sparked a shock of recognition and at least one story about the person pictured or their relatives. But the real treat in the selection was for John.

It was the first one I'd printed, the scene at the old Lame Deer flour mill. "That's Tom," John said softly. "He's my brother. And that's Mr. Mitchell, the flour mill boss. Tom is loading flour onto the wagon, and Mr. Mitchell is writing it down." John looked at the photograph for a long time in silence, as if remembering something. Then he carefully laid the photograph on the table and said to me, "We didn't have a lot of cars back then. Everybody got around in wagons."

There was another silence while he moved his fingertip around the edges of the print, tracing its outline. "How much will you charge to fix all these pictures for us?"

And it was done; in less than ten minutes we agreed and shook hands, and I was charged with selecting the best three-hundred negatives from the collection for the first round of restoration. The process would include cleaning the negatives, pulling and mounting a good print from each, and providing protective storage containers for the finished work.

Half an hour later, Tom and I were on the road again, driving back to Missoula. But I was on yet another road to Lame Deer, a road I would have to take alone and in the dark. Over the next two years, in weekend and late-night darkroom marathons that I jammed inside my other work, I slowly assembled the fragments of another time.

It was a rare and strange privilege to take that road to Lame Deer. Many of the strangers who appeared to me in the dark through the magic of the developer steadily became familiar as they returned in various settings. Even though I didn't know their names or the significance of the context the photographer was framing, their connections became more and more apparent. As the collective portrait of an obviously intimate relationship between Marquis and the Cheyennes, the photographs were profound.

Beyond that, I had to make many more trips on the actual road to Lame Deer to learn the names and the stories and gain some understanding of Marquis and that time and its relationship to the Lame Deer I was beginning to know. In a metaphorical way, the two roads began to work together, images of the past and present informing each other as I began to photograph elders whose youth had been recorded in the Marquis collection.

As a bonus, over the course of those long days and nights in the darkroom, there were strangely personal moments when the images seemed to offer their messages directly. One in particular stayed with me.

I had worked far into the Missoula night, and as a last effort for the session I chose a negative of two Cheyenne children with their horse. The boy stood holding the halter; the girl sat on the broad back of a very sleepy gray mare. As the image progressed in the developer there was an odd familiarity in the quality of the light. I knew that light. It was a late afternoon light that happens that way only on the high plains in late June, and it bathes everything and everyone with an unmistakable shade of orange-gold. And there it was in the photograph, embracing two children and an old horse. For a moment, when it was fully developed in the tray, I was a child again, basking in that same light along the banks of the Sun River, not far from my boyhood home in Great Falls.

5

Somewhere inside a silent avalanche of memories the sun dropped, and the light shifted from pale white to gold. The living room seemed brighter. Irene held her cup in both hands and sipped slowly. Her face had softened some, the tears less willing to appear. The Polaroids on her lap were hidden beneath my portraits of Belle.

We sat quietly with our coffee, and I scanned the room again. I hadn't noticed before that it was nearly empty. My eyes paused at the spot where the small table had been, next to the front window. Irene had kept the picture of her daughter there, and after I started making portraits of the elders, she put my portrait of Alex Black Horse there as well. The couch was gone too, and the potted philodendron that had occupied the corner next to it. Even though she had said so, it suddenly struck me that Irene didn't really live here anymore.

"You can keep those portraits of Belle," I said. And while she thanked me and studied them again, I remembered how it was that Henry and I had become collaborators. I remembered how he led me into the world of Cheyenne elders.

Springtime came early in March that first year, and the air in Montana stayed balmy from then on. By June the snow was gone from the mountains, and Lame Deer was already very dry. I was reeling a bit from the speed at which I'd been incorporated into Lame Deer society. Tom had warned me, and yet he too was a little surprised by our assimilation into the home of Henry and Irene. They treated us like family, and it was getting hard to imagine my life without them circling close to its center.

But as summer approached, Tom presented a sobering problem. His acquaintance among the elders was limited to John

Woodenlegs, Grover Wolf Voice, and Belle Highwalking. He had lived on the reservation for just over a year, and his circle of friendships reflected the dynamics of familial life. Most Cheyennes stay within the bounds of their extended family, rarely visiting beyond it. Visitation is highly valued within one's circle, but it is considered rude just to "drop in" on folks you don't know. And so Tom really could be of no further assistance to me in compiling a photo gallery of elders.

It was obvious that I would need a different helper, preferably an older Cheyenne who was bilingual and could present me and my camera to the community with grace and respect. For sheer proximity, Henry was the obvious choice. Beyond his age and language skills, he had access to many families, several who knew him through his story-collecting for the tribe. Tom left it to me to approach Henry with the proposal. Although I was reluctant, I knew he was right. Henry and I would have to find our way to the task on our own terms, and I would have to ask in the Cheyenne way.

When June came and I was without new subjects, there was little choice. Tom and I made our usual rounds, visiting Grover and Belle, and at Belle's cabin I asked her if I could take some more pictures of her. Clearly puzzled by me and my persistent camera, she said, "You sure take a lot of pictures!" I added another of her to the portfolio, but I could not seem to muster the courage to ask Henry, and my uncertainty as to whether I even had a project didn't make the task easier. Finally, on the night before we had to return to Missoula, I decided to make the request indirectly and let Henry think about it until we returned the next month. I waited for an opening all evening but hedged and waffled until it was past bedtime. Tom had already settled in on the couch, and Henry and I were alone at the dining table.

We both stared into the tabletop as I began. "Henry, you remember when I first came down in January and Alex Black Horse came to visit while you and Tom were at the meeting?" He nodded and I waited for words. None came. I continued. "He has a good face." I waited again. He nodded again. Silence. We stared at the table. I offered the hook. "It might be a good idea to get a portrait of him sometime." He nodded again, and the silence was longer because I had nothing left. And then, as he got up to take his cup to the sink, he said, "You could ask him." He stretched, yawned, excused himself, and went to bed.

I sat at the table for a long time after that and tried to determine how many ways that conversation had been ambiguous—more than I could count, and there was no clue as to what had been communicated. I turned the light out and listened while sleep sounds filled the house. I gave up. It seemed clear he didn't want the job. He knew there was no way I could ask Alex Black Horse.

It was two weeks after the Fourth of July before Tom and I were on the road to Lame Deer again. I had pretty well dismissed the possibility of making more portraits, but Tom reminded me of the dynamics of decision-making on the reservation and assured me that something would happen.

For this trip we had decided on a longer route, taking U.S. 12 out of Helena through the Musselshell country to Roundup and Forsyth and then south to Colstrip and Lame Deer. We stopped so often for pictures that it was dusk when we finally arrived at Henry's house. He was alone; Irene was visiting her daughter. We drank coffee on the front porch and watched the hill across the road turn red, then pink, then blue, and waited in the dark for the cool breezes to come so we could sleep.

That sleep came easily and was deep. From it, I emerged slowly into the aromatic wonder of sizzling pork fat and was instantly a child again, snuggled in my bed on a Sunday morning, savoring the aroma of breakfast while still clinging to sleep and feeling the cool morning air against my nose and chin. But another perfume hovering at the edge of the dream teased me back, all the way from Great Falls to Lame Deer. It was a smell too delicious to be believed, a smell so full of promise that it dragged me to the table while I tried simultaneously to clothe my disoriented body.

Hot coffee was waiting, and before I could down the first sip, Henry placed the plate before me: two eggs over easy, four buttermilk pancakes—and two fresh rainbow trout panfried in bacon grease. Astonished by this gustatory revelation, which would certainly confirm my death and arrival in paradise, I could only ask where he got the trout. He responded by asking if two eggs were enough and if I needed more coffee. I made the appropriate response at last and stuffed myself.

But beneath my gluttonous afterglow I was puzzled by the gesture. Henry was clearly Irene's equal in the kitchen; they had, after all, managed a cafe off the reservation for a while. Even as Cheyenne hospitality, however, the feast seemed beyond the typical obligation to treat guests well. And then it was suddenly obvious. There were no trout on his or Tom's plate. Henry had remembered my talk of fly-fishing and fresh trout and had cooked this meal especially for me. And the why of it all came just as swiftly when, after I'd gorged myself, he casually asked, "Would you like to go visit Alex now?"

I was speechless all the way to Alex's house. Henry smirked occasionally but said nothing beyond giving directions as my car lurched through the dusty maze of roads whose identity and organization steadily diminished until they found chaos and then disintegrated some fifty yards away from the house. We parked on a level spot facing it and waited for the dust cloud that had followed us for miles to pass over. I looked at Henry. He looked straight ahead. We kept the silence.

Out in front of us, Alex Black Horse and his family sat in cool comfort beneath a canvas awning stretched between four posts set in the ground. Apart from one cottonwood tree and the shadow of the house, it provided the only shade, a priceless commodity when the July afternoon heat presses down hard and the wind gets lost somewhere out on the plains.

The family had just finished the noon meal. Two women carried some food into the house. We waited. They continued as if we weren't there. I watched the heat waves start to dance on the hood of the car. Deep inside the stifling stillness a grasshopper clicked and jumped. Henry didn't move for a very long time. When at last he got out, I followed, and we leaned our butts against the headlights. "I'll go talk to him. You wait here."

Henry paused a few yards away from the awning and began to speak to Alex. I kept myself from staring by surveying the house and yard but tried to keep Henry and the family in my peripheral vision. The house was of the same vintage as Grover's but had cedar board-and-batten siding. Several of the silvered battens hung loosely away from the boards, and all were weathered black and gold, some offering furtive openings to the interior. In the yard were a few fragments of agricultural enterprises from times long past: a hand plow rusted paper thin, part of a barbed-wire fence coiled loosely against one wooden post, and beyond the house and awning the remnants of a corral competing with the dry stand of prairie grass for dominance.

At last a small breeze broke the stillness and ruffled the canvas as Henry stepped beneath it. He took a dipperful of water from the large bucket on the table, sipped a little, and then splashed the remainder on the ground in portions, one for each of the four cardinal directions. Then followed more talk, easily ten minutes' worth. Alex listened to Henry's monologue and nodded and occasionally looked in my direction. Finally, Henry took another drink but this time returned the dipper immediately to the pail and walked back to the car.

"He wants to know where would be a good place." I looked back at the awning but Alex had already disappeared into the house. "He says he'll be ready in a minute."

As I finished taping the black sheet I used as a backdrop against the north side of the house, Alex rounded the corner, smiling, peyote fan in hand, sporting his best shirt and hat. I still had no idea how we would proceed but shook hands and invited him to sit. He watched with great interest as I set up the tripod and view camera and checked the Rolleiflex for backup. All the while, Henry steadily engaged him in conversation so that by the time I was ready, Alex had nearly deleted my presence. Henry's eyes found mine and asked in a fraction of a glance if this was what I had in mind. I nodded just as quickly and put my head beneath the viewing cloth. And then, once again, the Cheyenne language captured me. The word sounds merged with the light in the open shade and settled around us while the face on the ground glass shed its uncertainty and the man emerged.

I had seen him before, of course, at Henry's house that first night when I was alone with Irene. Now, as he and Henry talked, that same soft sound greeted me again. But beneath the focusing cloth another dimension presented itself, and I was captivated.

I lingered, under cover, unable to withdraw from that view of him—unguarded, comfortable with Henry's talk, unaware of my voyeurism. And then he stopped talking and looked straight into the camera. I was startled, as if caught peeking, but quickly focused the camera again and stepped from beneath the cloth. Alex continued to look at me until his eyes found mine and held them.

And then I lost track of everything. Somewhere in that timelessness I felt my finger release the shutter, but there was no more sensation or awareness until I found myself kneeling on the ground, packing the view camera into its box. I looked up and our eyes met again. He showed a mixture of sincere concern and sympathy as he spoke to me and Henry translated: "He says you have a lot of work for just one picture."

Alex chuckled and Henry covered his laughter with his hand while I surveyed the array of technology between us: a dozen sheet-film holders, three lenses, filters, view camera, tripod, two reflex cameras, light meter, boxes of film, lens cleaner and tissues, and, of course, the infamous baby oil. Point taken. I laughed out loud and then laughed some more when Henry said, "He wants to know if he can have some pictures for his grandchildren. Five or six would be fine."

I offered cigarettes to him and Henry. Alex took one but put it in his shirt pocket, and Henry refused as he always did—"No, I don't smoke"—took it anyway and put it in his pocket as well. I lit mine and said, "Tell him I'll bring a dozen." He did, and Alex beamed and shook my hand once, softly, and said thank you in English.

Back in the car, Henry was buoyant and had decided that we were a team equal to Butch and Sundance. After I double-checked my camera bag and found I had indeed exposed film, I agreed and asked him which one he was. He insisted on Paul Newman because "he's good looking like me!" He laughed loudly without putting his hand over his mouth to cover the gaps in his teeth, and then suggested we go visit Willis Medicine Bull and his wife, Annie. "He's an Old Man Chief now. You should get his picture. Hers too—she has new false teeth!" We laughed again and longer and drove on into what remains in my mind now as one long day on the reservation, even though our journey through the community of elders occupied many months.

Henry knew he was a medicine man but would never declare it beyond claiming Ice as his great-grandfather. After that timeless day with Alex had transformed itself into a single day in my memory, however, filled with all the others, I had to consider that his medicine was at work within each portrait sitting—maybe it was Ice working through him. Each time I was lost in the sound of the words and the universe of faces, and each time my consciousness returned as if from sleep and dream—the dream fading swiftly into amnesia against all my efforts to hold it. And each time I found myself robotically repacking my equipment as Henry and the elder of the moment conversed and smiled while I, the object of their amusement, tried to reorient myself to them and the world. To this day I do not remember the actual "taking" of any of those pictures.

Of course, I do not pretend to understand what the Cheyennes mean by "medicine," or how they experience it. Nevertheless, it is certain that these portraits would not exist without the presence of Henry Tall Bull, medicine man or not. And I was never more certain of it than on that long day of days when Alex Black Horse's face dissolved into those of Annie and Willis Medicine Bull, and she sported the dentures that were not only new but the only ones on the reservation, and Willis told again the story of his father and the stool specimen and laughed until the lines in his face made joyful canyons from the corners of his eyes to his neck. The echoes of his laughter transformed his face into that of Hestahae, deaf and mute since birth, to whom I watched Henry speak in signs, twice translating for me, always respectful of Hestahae, whose name means "belly button" or "twin." His anglicanized name was Donald Hollowbreast. The reservation's premier journalist, he had edited the *Birney Arrow* from 1959 to 1971. He was also well known as an artist who painted Cheyenne history on paper and canvas.

Hestahae sat before me in his peyote robe and watched Henry's hands and offered my camera the toothless smile of a child and the deep reflection of a peyote man. He laughed with Henry's hands and took mine gently when we said goodbye and left to find our way to the home of William Hollowbreast, who laughed until there were tears when his wife, Carrie, ran squealing into the house at the first sight of my camera. He kept the laughter in his eyes for the portrait and asked Henry if Tom Weist was going to use his words in the history of the Cheyenne people they were working on. Born in 1900, William Hollowbreast had been among the first to feel the sting of acculturation when he was a child. Tom did use his words:

> At the time, the Indian medicine ways were prohib-
> ited. Indian doctors were always afraid. The Sun
> Dance and these other ceremonies like the Animal
> Dance were not supposed to be held. They were going
> to have a big meeting in Lame Deer. At that meeting
> some of these people who joined these churches said
> they let their Indian ways go and were going to these

churches instead. These people that were baptized
talked against the native spiritual ways—they said it
was no good. At that meeting, that's the way these
churches brought it out—that the Cheyennes themselves said it was no good. My own grandfolks were
quite spiritual people—they used to sneak around to
go to different ceremonial doings. My grandfather
went to fast and he pierced himself in the chest and
tied himself to a tree way out in the hills to worship
God. He came back down and everybody fixed food
and ate with him. The way that the old folks prayed to
God was good. They prayed for all of us and the family—we all kind of grew up and were all kind of
healthy. We all had the fear that the policemen would
come and search and throw the Indian medicine in the
fire or in the river. The people really hid their medicine
and doctoring one another because some would tell
on one another. . . . Ceremonial ways were for good
health, or to stay together to be unified and also kind
of a renewal of the life of the people—to pray for the
whole group. I know this is the truth, it does help. I
know that myself . . . the people that pray and help
each other and now people go to prayer meetings and
they pray that way today and we know it helped in the
past and it's the same way today.

Henry and I remembered those words all the way to Albert Tall
Bull's house. As a chief and Sun Dance priest, Albert was always
going somewhere, helping people, finding cash for them, running
errands for old people. When Tom lived on the reservation, he was
forever finding Albert standing by his perpetually broken-down
car, in need of a ride to deliver important articles or food or just to
meet with someone and listen to his or her troubles. He was said
to be the only Sun Dance priest who really knew the traditional way
to put up the ceremony. When we arrived, he was on his way out,
hoping his car would start.

I let the reflection of the hills and trees in his glasses frame his
eyes, eyes that rarely looked inward but were always searching the
horizon of the community for where he should go next. He donned
his best beaded vest for the portrait so that he would be a pre-

sentable chief. And all the while, his good humor and cheer were unrelenting.

Since that day, I have thought of Albert often, especially when I first read the traditional "charge to chiefs" as it was presented in 1905 by two important men at that time, Bushy Head and De Forest Antelope, and recorded by the anthropologist George Dorsey. Its presuppositions and obligations require a willingness to serve that few if any of us could muster.

> Now, listen to me! When the old chiefs wore out, they appointed you to carry on their leadership. We who are here representing the sacred magicians of old and the sacred arrows and the sacred sun, earth and animals, have this day advised you and placed every man, woman and child of the Cheyenne tribe in your care. When it is necessary you will help not only your own tribe, but all other Indians. You have been appointed on account of your bravery, character and courage. In the future, you will cause no disturbance or help to cause a disturbance among your own people. If another member of the tribe kills your own brother, take your pipe and smoke it to the Great Medicine, and you will prevent disturbance. Do not notice your brother's murderer. If your young men look despairing and lonely, take your pipe and pledge yourself to perform the great Medicine-Arrow ceremony in order that the Great Medicine will bless you and your people, because of your remembrance of him.

Although chiefs are appointed for life, many cannot bear the responsibility and eventually resign. Even when his service is performed in good faith, the chief is often subject to the harangues of those who think he should give more, if only a glass of water and a sympathetic ear when times are hard. A chief is always penniless and without possessions. He gives everything away when asked and subsists within the circle of reciprocity. Henry and I gave Albert a ride into Busby that day. I paid him ten dollars for the sitting. I saw him give it to a woman on the porch of the Busby store as he went in.

Ernest King, also named Ernest Mexican Cheyenne, looked up over my shoulder at the hill above Lame Deer and the spire of the Mennonite church. He had been a devout Mennonite all his adult life. He and the other elder members of the congregation were the converts of the reservation's first Mennonite missionary, Rudolfe Petter.

Petter first established a mission in 1891 among the Southern Cheyennes in Oklahoma. Already multilingual, he was soon fluent in Cheyenne and began codifying the language. When he visited Montana in 1899, the Northern Cheyennes were astonished to hear him preach in fluent Cheyenne.

Petter liked Montana and by 1911 had persuaded the church to allow him to continue his mission in Lame Deer. There he continued the task of codifying the language. He translated the New Testament into Cheyenne, published a grammar and a hymnal, and embarked on the monumental task of compiling a Cheyenne-English dictionary—a labor of love that occupied him until his death in 1947. Ernest King, with Anna Wolfname, was instrumental in completing the dictionary.

But beyond linguistics, Petter's influence brought converts to the ministry itself. Through his support and guidance several Cheyennes studied and became evangelists, notably, Frank Little Wolf and Milton Whiteman. When Ernest King sat for a portrait session with me, Joe Walks Along was pastor of the Petter Memorial Church in Lame Deer.

Petter's evangelism was successful in converting many Cheyennes to Christianity largely because the tenets of the Mennonite faith, which celebrates material simplicity and rejects all secular authority as well as the enforced baptism of infants (which Cheyennes also feared and rejected), were closer to traditional Cheyenne spiritual values. And Petter's validation of their language reflected a stance relative to Cheyenne culture that was less pejorative than that of the other Christian denominations with their persistent emphasis on English, Latin, and sin. In the end, though, it was Rudolfe Petter the man who won their hearts. He and his wife are buried in the Lame Deer cemetery. Ernest King spoke well of him that day as he looked up and over my shoulder at Rudolfe Petter's church while I took his photograph.

Lockwood Standing Elk, aged ninety-one and blind, sat before me in a withered aluminum lawn chair and chatted easily with Henry while I taped the backdrop to the log wall behind him and set up the camera. His grandson, who had helped him from the house, hovered at the side of the building and smiled continuously as the old man talked. Given his age, he would have been born at the beginning of the reservation period and heard firsthand accounts of the Custer fight, the Fort Robinson escape, and the march north. His elders had been the lords of the plains, and he, like Willis Medicine Bull, was now one of the four Old Man Chiefs. Lockwood's Cheyenne name was Bird Nest.

A real chief will always deny that he is one, and so you can be sure that if someone tells you he is a chief, he's pulling your leg or just plain lying. He must exemplify the quality of modesty and so cannot claim his status. Knowledge of it must come from another, just as his election must come from tribal consensus. "Old Man Chiefs" are the highest representatives of the standard. And in a political system where establishing consensus often turns on the decision of an elder, the Old Man Chief receives final deference, since he has proved that he has the best interests of the people at heart.

I sat back on my haunches and looked at the eyes that saw only memories, and for the first time I remained conscious for the sitting. The more Standing Elk talked, the more he chuckled and laughed, until his grandson and Henry were overcome by it all. I had clicked the shutter merrily along the waves of his mirth and was reloading the Rolleiflex when Henry finally decided to share the wealth.

"He says that the young kids think they're smart. They get allotment check, hitch a ride to Billings on Saturday morning, buy a $250 weekend special, get drunk, wreck the car by Sunday night, hitch a ride back to the reservation, broke on Monday morning. Next month, they do it all again! He thinks it's funny—they never figure it out. Those cars are no damned good!"

When Henry finished translating, Lockwood belly-laughed again and then softened. He spoke quietly to his grandson, who asked if I had enough pictures; the old man, he said, got tired quickly. He listened again to his grandfather and then said to me, "He says he wants to go in now." I took Lockwood's outstretched hand and thanked him. When he held on and pulled himself up, reaching behind for his grandson, I was astonished at his strength. Henry looked at me and was clearly satisfied. "He says he is ninety-one years old, but I think he's older. It's good we saw him. He's an important man."

I'd had the peculiar sensation for some time that we were being observed. But it wasn't until Lockwood and his grandson had entered the house that I turned around and confronted the stares of two small children, deeply entranced by my battery of equipment. When I faced them, the girl skittered out of sight. The boy remained, fascinated by my Rolleiflex. I offered it to him, and he cautiously approached. As he tried viewing Henry through the ground glass he said, "My grandmother lives right over there." He motioned to the rear with his head, the camera still plastered against his eye. "You should take her picture too!" He handed back the camera, moved away, and motioned for me to follow. I looked at Henry. He said, "I think I know her."

We followed the crest of the hill and then dropped down a little to a small plateau overlooking the valley. The boy had disappeared, but by the time we reached the tiny log cabin, Bessie Elkshoulder had emerged and was standing in front of the door. Henry did know her and immediately greeted her and asked if she would sit for me. She laughed her version of Lockwood's belly laugh, a staccato cackle two octaves higher and twice as fast, then said something with a decidedly mysterious tone and laughed again, even faster and higher. Henry translated the warning: "She says lots of white men have taken her picture but their films always come out blank!" I laughed a different kind of laugh and looked anxiously into my camera bag. The single roll of film in the Rollei was all I had left—twelve exposures.

She sat on a short bench in front of the cabin wall while I taped up the backdrop and Henry engaged her in conversation. I found her face in the ground glass and made three exposures while trying to find the angle that would allow her eyes to emerge through lenses thick as the bottoms of Coke bottles. I tried two more before I asked Henry to ask her to remove her glasses. When she did, I was overwhelmed by the transformation. And then her warning about white men and blank film returned like a curse. I had just seven frames remaining, and she had already told me that my mission was a lost cause. Her maiden name, Wandering Medicine, was suddenly and profoundly relevant.

I could hear nothing but her laughter ringing inside my head, and then the seven frames were gone and I just stood there, dazed, wondering how long it would be before I found the guts to develop the film. Bessie was unfazed by the whole affair, but she froze along with the rest of us as a shriek shattered the afternoon and a woman followed it out of the cabin amid a cloud of dust and a hailstorm of invective.

She directed it all at Henry, screaming in Cheyenne, punctuating the long arches of hostility with English repetitions of "Goddamn BIA!" and "Goddamn Tribal Council!" The children scurried behind her, their wide eyes peering out at us from the darkness just inside the cabin door. Bessie rose slowly from the bench and walked silently past her as she continued, drowning out Henry's meager attempts to respond. Not until she caught her breath after a particularly long burst did he manage a solid counterstatement. Without a flinch she hurled another short but withering barrage and then made her own dust devil as she spun back into the house.

We had been effectively chastised, and though I'd missed the specifics, I got the point. Back in the car I winced and squirmed in the silence. Henry was obviously embarrassed and tried to explain that she was mad at him, not me. "She said I shouldn't be collecting stories, and since John Woodenlegs had been tribal chairman, he should pay the families of the elders who gave stories to the research association. And nobody asked the old people in her family for stories and that was my fault because I'm probably working for the BIA and getting paid twice." Henry shook his head and chuckled a little. "Boy, she sure was mad, huh." I nodded and was grateful for his deference as I watched his face darken and felt him retreat inward.

As if to make sure we didn't forget our day with Bessie Elkshoulder, her daughter's dust devil caught up to us and whipped through the open windows as I turned the car back toward Lame Deer. Henry's eyes, narrowed against the assault of dust and sun, were fixed on the horizon. When we got back to the house, Tom was waiting on the porch. "I hope he has a cold one for me— might have to go to Jimtown otherwise." Tom did and handed the can to him just as his foot hit the porch. Henry stayed at home while we went to visit George Highwalker.

It was a late summer afternoon when I made the portrait of George Highwalker, and I was worried about the light. Indeed, the photograph did prove to be slightly underexposed, and making a good print is tricky. Yet these complications could not subdue the overwhelming masculinity he presented. His athletic body and "bad

boy" good looks belied his sixty-five years. He exuded virility and
was the kind of man whose natural strength and toughness were
tempered by a calm assurance that attracted women and com-
manded the respect of men. But he was more than a ladies' man; in
the old days he would have been a warrior, one who was eloquent,
knowledgeable, and skillful as a hunter and leader of men.

George Highwalker was a lover, but within Cheyenne culture
that status represents a rich complexity. Cheyenne sexuality is
not about immorality or rampant promiscuity. Rather, as the early
accounts of white explorers reveal, the Cheyennes have traditionally been a people of high moral aspirations who prize the chastity
of their unmarried women and the devotion of elders to their
spouses. Before the Christians came, some men took more than
one wife, but the general trend was toward monogamy. In the end
the Cheyennes are, like most human societies, mildly polygamous
(i.e., about half the population have multiple spouses in series).

And so love, marriage, and divorce are matters of complexity
heightened by the intricacies of Cheyenne familism and reciprocity. Indeed, that complexity, coupled with the high moral tone of
their religious beliefs, makes infidelity and divorce the subjects of
lasting stigma and pain. Yet the post–World War II rise in alcoholism, the relentless grind of poverty, and disenchantment with
tradition in many of the youth increased the divorce rate on the
reservation—a disturbing phenomenon for the elder community
for whom monogamy had been the norm and divorce the painful
exception.

George Highwalker was a lover, and his wife had recently divorced him for several reasons but mostly because other women
found him as attractive as she did and he responded in kind. He'd
had his run with alcohol as well but was sober for the time being.
Although he and his wife had been separated for more than a year,
he still wasn't handling it well. When Tom and I went to visit him
that day, they'd been divorced only a few months, and George was
still getting used to his new bachelorhood. His mother, Belle Highwalking, had enjoyed some fifty years of marriage to a man who
never strayed. For her, divorce was unthinkable. She wasn't speaking to George at all. His response to her silence and to the usual
reservation gossip was to live as far away from Lame Deer and
Busby as he could.

Tom, of course, was well acquainted with the story. He and George had become good friends when Tom lived in Lame Deer and George's wife, Helen, was translator for the writing project and a prominent force in the bilingual program. Tom and Tobie had listened patiently during the breakup and had tried to maintain a supportive low profile while continuing contact with all parties concerned, pleading ignorance when the gossip came to them. He knew we would hear it all again when we arrived at George's place.

As we rounded the base of a hill the cabin emerged slowly, tucked neatly against the hillside beneath a grove of cottonwoods, the front yard dominated by a large corral for working horses. George met us on the porch; coffee was brewing while he and Tom spoke quietly of Helen and his persistent hope that she would come back to him. Finally, hope and heartbreak gave in to talk about the good old days, and George at last began to brighten.

He had come of age on the crest of the first time in reservation history when the Cheyennes enjoyed some prosperity and the hope of self-sufficiency as stockmen. They had begun in 1903 with a herd of one thousand cows and forty bulls (grace of the U.S. Department of the Interior), and the men, already superior horsemen, found it easy to become cowboys. By 1912 the herd had grown to twelve thousand, and regular shipments of Cheyenne stock were bringing top dollar in Chicago. The Cheyennes were enjoying economic security, but it was not to last.

Local white ranchers, jealous and land hungry, complained to the government. They accused the Cheyennes of undercutting them at market and called for an investigation. The Montana Stockman's Association finally convinced government officials that the Cheyennes were overgrazing and mismanaging their herds. And so in 1914 the Department of the Interior took over the management of the Cheyenne cattle business. Under its direction, the herd dwindled to less than four thousand head. Completely ignorant of the dynamics of open-range cattle management, government range bosses left thousands of cattle to die of exposure on open ridges in winter.

By 1924 the government deemed the project a failure, sold the remaining stock at auction, and leased two large tracts totaling 143,000 acres of prime grazing land to two white ranchers, who paid ten cents an acre for the privilege—half the price of comparable land off the reservation. Once again impoverished, the

Cheyennes were forced to accept the land allotment program that placed most of their land "in trust" for the next forty years.

By the time George was a young man, the Cheyenne cattle business was over. But he'd become a cowboy anyway, and since there was little stock to tend, he joined the rodeo circuit as a bronc rider and trick roper. He'd found his niche, and in 1939 he became the first Native American to win the competition for World Champion Cowboy and Trick Roper.

It was small justice, but it may have been worth the price of the lost herd just to see those Montana stockmen squirm as they watched their cowboy image suffer an identity crisis when in 1939 the Indian wearing the white hat was named best cowboy. George Highwalker had the championship belt buckle to prove it. When he handed it to me for inspection, its silver and gold shone as brightly as the day he got it and, Cheyenne modesty not withstanding, so did his eyes.

He didn't hesitate when I asked to take his portrait and was in and out of the house in seconds. With the belt buckle as the pièce de résistance, he filled out his ensemble with stiff new jeans, a pearl-buttoned black shirt, and a buff-white straw hat. The Champion made his entrance graciously to a chorus of catcalls and whistles from Tom. As he sat before me, his sixty-five years regressed beneath the emergent elegance that surely had been George Highwalker in 1939. Here was a beautiful man, and for those few seconds when I saw him through the ground glass, he gave me an image of a kind of manhood and a freedom of spirit I imagined once dominated the plains.

George Highwalker was a lover and he was equally a showman. When the sitting was finished, he quickly fetched his ropes from the house and asked if I'd like to see a few tricks, "maybe take some pictures too." He positioned himself in front of the corral as he had when he'd received the prize, as if waiting for the announcement from the loudspeaker—his distorted hand the only sign of age.

There followed an awesome display of spinning ropes and cowboy gymnastics which I rode, dodged, and wove through while pumping the shutter as fast as I could. It was spectacular but brief. Breathless, he bent over with his hands on his knees and complained about his age to mask the searing arthritic spasms in his legs. Then, as if nothing had happened, he straightened and smiled and asked if I needed him to repeat anything. When I assured him

I'd got it all, he beamed and wiped the dust from his belt buckle with a clean white handkerchief.

When we turned to leave, he asked Tom to speak to Helen for him, to let her know he wanted her to come back: "She would listen to you." Tom waffled but finally placated him with "I'll see what I can do." George nodded. He was leaning against the corral rail and methodically coiling the crisp white ropes as we drove away.

The car turned sharply around the hill that eclipsed his house, and I was suddenly reluctant to leave, distressed that I hadn't secured an agreement that we would meet again or, worse yet, the deeper agreement that would move us toward a long friendship. By the time we hit the main road, I knew I wanted that friendship as much as I knew it wasn't going to happen.

He was the kind of man who drew you to him, yet as the hill shielding his house merged with every other hill on the plains, I could not ignore the fact of his remoteness, his unavailability—as if his was a land apart. Somehow he had stepped away from the network of kinship and still further from the circle of elders. Even his house, located away from relatives, had melancholy and loneliness about it.

George Highwalker was alone. And in the communal world of families that is the Cheyenne world, this is an unthinkable position. For thousands of years, including their last nomadic days on the plains, the Cheyennes traveled and lived together. Individuals rarely ventured out alone. The romanticized Hollywood image of the individualistic warrior represents a person who never existed. This is why the vision quest or the solitary fast at the sacred mountain are such fantastic and important experiences for the Cheyenne people. To be left alone on the plains in the old days was an invitation to death, not by beasts but by human enemies. Exile, therefore, was a fate worse than death. Of course no one had formally "exiled" George, yet I could not banish the feeling that exile was his condition. I had sensed it with Henry as well, on that February morning when I took his picture and felt the scars beneath my fingers and caught that distant look in his eyes.

Those feelings persisted as we pulled up in front of Henry's house. It was dusk and the lights were on in the kitchen. I saw Irene through the open door and felt a sudden relief. I was uneasy about drinking with Henry and deeply ambivalent about the stigma, too often a reality, of the drunk Indian.

We had already quenched one hot July afternoon with a six-pack, and on that first occasion Tom and I glossed the issue. Tom said, "I don't mind a beer now and then." In keeping with current political correctness, I refused to accept the prejudice from genetics that Indians can't hold their liquor; I blamed the problem historically on the whiskey traders and currently on reservation problems. I even quoted Benjamin Franklin, who had praised rum as "the appointed means by which the design of providence to extirpate these savages was fulfilled in order to make room for the cultivators of the earth." I said it with appropriate disdain but worried anyway. The loneliness I saw in George and Henry and their unspecified exile, perhaps from manhood itself, was too conducive to drink and the final loneliness of the alcoholic. And so I was glad to see that Irene was back and that Henry was sober. We ate luxuriously and told stories and talked about going to visit Josie Limpy in the morning.

The dirt road that runs southeast along Lame Deer Creek for a while continues on its own to Birney Village, where Josie Limpy lived. Tom and Henry wanted me to see the infamous "Birney Ditch," the permanent landmark of the Tongue River Irrigation Project, whose failure ran parallel to that of the Cheyenne cattle business in the first two decades of the century. As an engineering fiasco it has few parallels and provides ample demonstration of what can happen when the Army Corps of Engineers and the Bureau of Indian Affairs join forces in the name of public works. Henry loved the story.

The project began genuinely enough when in 1902 the reservation agent, J. C. Clifford, stated the obvious in his annual report: "Without water it is impossible to grow crops of any kind successfully; past years of failures have fully demonstrated that fact to the settlers in this part of the country. Where the white settlers can not make success out of farming without water, it can not be expected that the Indians can."

After four years of urging by Clifford, the project got under way in 1907 near Birney Village. During the first summer's work, three floods destroyed large sections of the canal and several gate structures. The next spring, ice jams in the Tongue River caused major floods that destroyed several canals and headgates. Nevertheless, by 1910 the canal system had been completed at a cost of $160,000.

It irrigated some five-hundred acres at over three-hundred dollars per acre—a small fortune for the times—and twenty-four families began cultivating the irrigated land. The main canal, however, failed to sustain an adequate water level, and its smaller branches proved subject to cave-ins due to seepage after spring rains and runoff. Finally, the seepage spread surface alkali throughout the soil, spoiling all the adjacent land and, of course, the newly planted crops. In 1913 another flood partially destroyed the primary headgate and further degraded other canals.

In 1915, John A. Buntin replaced Clifford as agent and began to disengage from the irrigation project by discontinuing the practice of "ditch riding" as the basis for general maintenance of the canals. The system quickly fell into disrepair, and by 1918 most of it had been abandoned. By 1920, with the original five-hundred acres completely destroyed by alkali seepage, the last of the twenty-four families had abandoned their farms. The Birney Ditch, however, remains—a barren reminder of the progress of Indian acculturation. Henry laughed out loud when Tom said, "If you want it done wrong, just hire the Corps of Engineers and have the BIA supervise!"

We all got out of the car and peered into the ditch. Henry walked along the edge for a bit and then climbed a small hill. I scanned the area and looked out into the Tongue River basin. Out there were many places for good campsites. The ditch itself was overgrown with sage brush and looked, apart from its size, like any other Montana dry-wash. We followed Henry up the hill to get a broader view of the ditch and the basin.

Henry said that in the old days a Cheyenne camp seen from a hill like this would have shown the circular arrangement of tipis typical of Plains tribes. But the Cheyenne circle was always incomplete, with an opening in the arc that faced east, as did the doorways to each of the lodges. They were placed that way to greet the spirit of the east, who came each morning with the sun to bring blessings and the gift of life to the people.

Within the open circle, set apart from the other lodges, the people placed the Sacred Tipi, so that it too opened to the east. Every springtime, the time of renewal, the people brought newly tanned skins to re-dress the lodge and appropriately decorate it. Then, one by one, the adult males were called to enter the tipi and view the sacred objects: the Sacred Buffalo Hat and medicine

bundles. If they were in good condition, the keepers of the Sacred
Tipi had been faithful, and the well-being of the tribe was assured
for another year.

These sacred objects and their ceremonial functions are unique
to the Cheyenne people (unlike the Sun Dance, which is shared by
nearly all Plains tribes) and central to their religion and way of life.
They have been well cared for from the beginning and remain
within the care of present-day keepers on the Northern Cheyenne
reservation in Montana. Tom and Henry talked about the office of
Keeper of the Sacred Tipi which, like all official positions, is elec-
tive. The similarity ends there, however, because once selected the
chosen one may not refuse. (Of course, the chosen one initially re-
sponds with a pro forma refusal, because to do otherwise would reveal undesirable character.) The choice is made by the entire community with direction from the chiefs, who guide the selection
away from those who have great accomplishments as warriors
or potential as leaders. What is sought, rather, is a purity of character that is above the realm of communal politics and the heroics
of combat.

The Keeper therefore represents pure altruism. His sacrifice is,
in essence, himself, since his office traditionally prohibits participation in the normal rounds of tribal life. In the old days the
Keeper did not hunt, engage in warfare, or do manual work of any
kind beyond maintenance of the Sacred Tipi. The people were
obliged to bring gifts of food and clothing to him (and his wife if
he had one). Although entirely dependent upon the tribe for his
sustenance, he could not demand it or evaluate its quality. Con-
versely, he was not expected to "give away" or offer gifts.

With the advent of the reservation, however, practical survival
issues diminished the people's ability to provide adequately for the
Keeper and his family. Often destitute, embarrassed and overwhelmed by their lack of support, early reservation Keepers were
forced to seek casual labor in order to continue their sacred obligation. Since the turn of the century they have largely supported
themselves. Their election, however, remains a matter of the most
important concern, as is the status of the Sacred Buffalo Hat and
the medicine bundles.

I asked Tom and Henry if they knew what was in the sacred bundles. Henry said he didn't know, but Tom said that in 1959, Head
Swift, then Keeper of the Sacred Tipi, opened the bundles for three

non-Cheyennes to view: Margot Liberty, Ann Hanks, and Father
Peter J. Powell. A large hide sack contained a bundle of braided
sweet grass tied with a red cloth, several offering cloths, and five
scalps, laced to wooden hoops, which were supposedly taken
from their traditional enemies: the Pawnees, Apaches, Utes, Sho-
shones, and Crows. A smaller hide sack contained a package of
nineteenth- century trade tobacco in long twists, an ancient mink
or otter hide, a bundle of what was said to be the wool of a yellow
buffalo calf wrapped in a yellow checkered cloth, and, of course,
the Sacred Buffalo Hat (the upper part of a buffalo's skull with the
hair and horns intact).

Head Swift was Josie Limpy's father, and after he died, when no
suitable male candidate could be found, Josie was elected temporary Keeper. In this way the Cheyennes demonstrate the complexity of their religious philosophy, which is by no means "sexist" as
we understand the term. Women are not excluded from ceremonial
practice because of inferiority or because they might do harm or
because their presence is in any way heretical. Rather, it is believed
that as representatives of the earth, their value must be placed elsewhere. It is not inconsistent with Cheyenne beliefs that a woman
could be elected Keeper of the Sacred Buffalo Hat when no male
met the prerequisites of character. In Josie Limpy's case, moreover,
precedent extended beyond her father, back to the middle of the
nineteenth century: her grandfather, Coal Bear, and her great-
grandfather, Half Bear, had also been Keepers.

We returned to the car and drove slowly into Birney Village. After all that musing out there on the plains, imagining the look of a
traditional village, the town was an abrupt reminder of how times
had changed. From one main street containing a store and a gas
station a somewhat random arrangement of housing fanned out.
As in Lame Deer, there was the mix of pre-fabs on platted streets
with clusters of older houses and cabins.

I thought about the Keeper's dependence on the tribe for sustenance in the early days as I looked at the tipi next to Josie Limpy's
pre-fab house. The Sacred tipi needed some help, but it looked
more out of place than run down. What had once been the focal
point of a Cheyenne village was oddly relocated, ordinary, just another structure among many: a tipi in a vacant lot next to a pre-fab
house on a side street in a small Montana town.

We got out of the car and paused in front of the Sacred Tipi. I respectfully did not make a photograph. Henry said, "I'll see if she's home."

Tom and I waited near the car while Henry knocked and then talked at the narrow opening of the door to a face we could barely see. At last the door opened wider, and the face of a middle-aged Cheyenne woman peered at us for a moment, nodded, smiled, and then disappeared within. Henry turned to us and said, "She needs a minute to ask Josie if it's all right."

At last the door opened wide, and the woman stepped out to greet us. Henry introduced Tom and me as we went in; she followed, chattering vigorously at Henry until we entered the small kitchen, where she paused briefly for introductions. Josie was fussing a little with her hair. Her companion quickly resumed her conversation with Henry in Cheyenne while she cast quick glances at me and giggled more and more as I fumbled with the backdrop.

Josie was quietly amused and cooperative as I posed her near the only window in the room. Henry put her at ease, while I got nervous. The light didn't seem right; there was too much side light. I repositioned her chair and adjusted the backdrop. Josie's friend laughed, and Josie said something to Henry, and then he laughed while I adjusted the backdrop again.

"She says you worry too much."

She grinned at me, and I agreed and took a breath.

"She wants to know if she can have a picture for her granddaughter."

I said "Of course, as many as she likes." She grinned even wider when he translated, and I at last settled down.

In the car heading back to Lame Deer, I knew I'd made the portrait but was again beset with amnesia. I thought about what Henry had said about Spirit People, medicine men and women, and how it's believed that they have special powers and access to uncommon knowledge. Henry had also said that the Keepers of the Sacred Hat are chosen because they have purity of character. I wondered if I had felt that when I was with Josie. I wondered if that was why I couldn't remember anything this time. Something new had happened, unlike my amnesia after previous sessions with elders.

Later, of course, the finished portraits of Josie Limpy at least confirmed the event. I looked at them and was convinced that I must have experienced Josie Limpy's special powers, her medicine. I remembered what Henry had said, that when the wars on the plains were over and the Cheyenne way changed forever, everybody believed the medicine of the Sacred Hat went dormant. He said the medicine men believe that one day the powers of the Sacred Hat will return and restore the natural order. When he was a little boy some holy people told him that when the sacred powers came back, the world would be the way it was before the white man came. I thought about that and wondered about my amnesia. Josie Limpy had obviously fulfilled her responsibility to the sacred objects of her people, and Henry would have said she gave me amnesia to protect them.

I had long since lost faith in saints and mysticism. Certainly, I had no reference for what the Cheyennes mean by "medicine." Perhaps Henry was right, but in the end, all my wonderings were resolved within their faces, the faces of Josie Limpy and all the elders who allowed me to look at them in that strangely invasive photographer's way. And in doing so, each of them demonstrated style and grace I shall never forget.

6

Irene and I were silent. It was almost noon. We had, at last, spoken long and well, but now our silence meant that the visit was about to end. She took my portrait of Henry from the stack on her lap and looked at it.

And then she looked at me. Her eyes were clear. No tears were coming. Our eyes met and held us silently. And then she looked down at the picture again, and my mind was flooded by the long sequence of days that had ended on yet another last day, a day I knew I could never speak about with her, the last day I spent as a guest in her house. A day like this one, where I played and replayed all the events leading up to it over and over in my mind, trying and failing to make sense of it all.

But as I sat with her and remembered that sequence, I also knew I would never forget those days, for they contained everything I would cherish about my friendship with Henry. Indeed, the first of those days was surely the one where Tom and Henry and I had come to regard our friendship as eternal.

We had settled into the routine we loved best—wandering the open spaces around the reservation in search of the curious and strange. Henry loved finding geological and architectural oddities for me to photograph, and Tom was willing to test his Volvo's mettle against anything those back roads had to offer. We had no agenda except to discover what might await us just beyond the next hill. And what we found there was often strange and curious indeed— like the place we came to call the Bone Ranch.

In keeping with our agenda, we had found it by accident. Even Henry was surprised by its existence and was clearly spooked by its appearance in a place that should have been empty. Indeed, the spot was barren and without any history of planting, even a family garden. The buildings had been placed, with no apparent design in mind, in a slight depression on an otherwise level plain. When we stepped out of the car, the sky darkened—a cosmic response that added an appropriate touch of menace to the scene. Henry looked anxiously at the sky.

The house was set down into the earth like a sod house with but two feet between the windowsills and the ground and a very low-pitched roof. We had to step down and stoop to enter a door that had stood open for decades. Inside, my head brushed the rafters.

It was mostly kitchen. The remainder, beneath the peak, was a bedroom on the ground floor with a sleeping loft above it. Only a suspended stovepipe remained where the cooking had been done. A thick layer of dust covered the clay slip floor as well as the table and chairs. These, still in place and arranged for seating, fronted five place settings barely visible beneath the fine powder. Each was correctly set, as if ready for a meal about to be served. I reached down and brushed away the dust. The plate was clean. I felt the hair rise a little on the back of my neck and looked at Tom. We both looked for Henry. He hadn't followed us. A rafter creaked and released a sifting of dust that drew a fine line down the center of the table. We made a quick exit.

Outside, the harsh gray sky was close to the ground, and Henry was nowhere to be seen. The broad expanse around the house and barn was vacant but for a large, eight-by-eight post. Oddly reminiscent of a medieval pillory, it was five feet high with a steel plate near the top that had once secured a heavy ring. Beneath the plate was a series of deeply etched marks in a herring-bone pattern, clearly made by an ax. I suddenly lurched into consciousness and remembered why I was there by trying to frame the barn in the ground glass. Tom nudged my arm and pointed to the ground.

In every direction the earth was littered with bones, mammal bones: femurs, ulnas, ribs, partial pelvic bones, unidentifiable bones, and fragments of bones. We stood up with bones in our hands and scanned the area for Henry.

I was about to call him when he seemed to pop out of the side of the little rise opposite the house. He moved very slowly, backward, and we saw that he was exiting a small vestibule embedded in the hillside. Its door hung from one hinge and was open wide, almost plastered against the hill. The vestibule extended about three feet out from the hill and had an elegant pitched roof with shingles.

Once clear of the door, Henry did a quick turn and marched double-time toward us.

As he approached, his face slowly revealed that rare and infrequently documented phenomenon, the pale-faced Indian. En route to the car, he didn't look at us or break his stride: "There's a deer in there!" We heard the car door slam and lock as we dropped our bones and moved out toward the hillside.

Inside the vestibule, another door led to an interior room, a once ornate Dutch door whose upper half had exploded away, leaving the opening filled with the rotting corpse of a whitetail buck. His forelegs were hooked over the lower half, his body angled upward. He'd obviously sought shelter in the room during the winter and had tried to vault out of the room when the earth caved in behind him and buried him up to his shoulders. It had taken him a long time to die. One of his eyes had completely rotted away, but the other, still firm and lustrous, was filled with struggle and anguish.

I lingered outside and contemplated the gingerbread design in the facia over the door. Its ornate scrolls seemed oddly out of step with the crude Honyocker architecture of the house and barn. I turned and saw Tom standing across the yard in front of a pile of garbage. When I joined him, he was chuckling to himself and shaking his head.

"There's nothing but catsup bottles here—hundreds of them!" He was right; there were hundreds of them, the antique, green glass variety with the brand name cast in bas-relief. We looked incredulously at each other and began to assemble the clues: the bones, the killing post, the sanctuary in the hillside, the fateful "last supper." They wouldn't sum, really, but suggested a gothic if not murderous scenario. "Whatever they were eating, it needed a lot of catsup," he said as he pitched a bottle back on the pile and turned toward the car.

Henry was all but invisible—just the top of his head showed along the lower lip of the back window—and was slow to respond when we tapped on the door. The keys were locked in the car with him. We could hold our laughter no longer when he finally released the lock. I slid in and heard him hiss "*Mestaae'a*" (spook) at us. He stayed slouched down in the seat until the Bone Ranch was well out of sight.

Before we got back to Lame Deer, Tom had cracked enough catsup jokes to get Henry upright and laughing, but he was still a little spooked and leery of us. Cheyennes won't go near the bones of the dead and we had handled them and they could have been human. In any case, the place seemed clearly haunted by all manner of *Mestaae'a*, as the trapped deer demonstrated. Nonetheless, by the time we had consumed one of Irene's culinary masterpieces and were sitting around the table in the twilight and drinking beer, Henry had reframed the experience sufficiently to scare the bejeezus out of Irene with his own ghoulish speculations about the secrets of the Bone Ranch. She squealed in terror at every detail and could not believe that Tom and I had actually touched the bones. She teased and called us *Mestaae'a*, because only spooks will touch dead things. Henry looked spooked again when I told him I wanted to go back, confessing that I'd failed to take many pictures because of the strangeness of the place.

Of course, ghost stories became the theme for the night, and ghost stories go better in the dark. The day had been unbearably hot, and I understood well the Montana summer strategy of sitting in the dark until the earth cools down. But when midnight came and with it the steady flow of cool breezes and the lights did not come on even when someone went to the bathroom, I was puzzled. And we were out of ghost stories. Irene saw what I was thinking and quickly acknowledged it.

"Jerry's wondering why we're still sitting in the dark," she said and then spoke directly to me. "If we don't, the tribal cops might see us drinking. It's three days in the tribal jail if you get caught. Henry doesn't like it there!" He laughed and said, "It's not so bad. I know all the police. I served all of them beer when I used to tend bar in Jimtown."

I began to launch a proper tirade on the vagaries of prohibition when three rapid and very loud knocks at the front door cut me off.

No one spoke. I knew we were busted. And then another knock, this time followed by a whisper hissing at us under the door: "Henry! Irene! It's Vernon! Let me in, let me in!"

We took a collective deep breath and Henry went to the door. Then we froze again when he released the latch and the door flew open, nearly knocking him over as a shadowy creature vaulted into the room on all fours, gasping and spitting orders. "Quick! Close the door! Close the door! The cops are after me!"

We froze again while approaching headlights flashed across the front window, and we listened to the engine slow, then idle briefly in front of the house, and finally accelerate into the night. As we released an explosion of laughter and relief and greetings, Vernon stood up and handed Henry a six-pack. "Thanks, Henry, he's been chasing me all over Lame Deer for an hour!"

He was tall, well over six feet, but seemed even taller in the dark. His thick, muscular torso was like his father's; his face softer, yet dark with the same undercurrents. He introduced himself to Tom and me, and then we all settled again around the table, and with each fresh beer the talk became more intimate: after-hours talk among the regulars at their private tavern of the night. And soon, as we loosened and talked our way toward personal disclosure, the conversation became Vernon's story.

"My son," Henry said. "He's a warrior—did two tours in Vietnam." His speech was thick with beer, and Vernon stiffened a little when his father's arm wrapped and squeezed his shoulders. "He's a warrior . . . " Vernon pushed his arm off, clearly embarrassed. "Henry, cut it out!—gimme another beer."

Vernon began where he was, which was where he had been for over a year, which was deep within the endless repetition of nine walks up and nine walks down some anonymous hill somewhere around My Lai, where death could not take him. Each time he saw death precisely take those to his right, those to his left. Each time he felt the heat as the bullets passed around his body; each time he felt the coolness of death pass him by—once, twice, three times—until after the fourth or fifth charge he stepped over the line at the edge of the world of the Dog Soldier and the suicide warrior. Once there, he let go of all defense and aggression and began to walk up the hill in a full upright position, facing the unseen enemy, rifle dangling from its strap, his eyes seeing nothing, his ears hearing only the dull rumble of war and the high whine of enemy ordinance curving around him—up and down again and again until his final descent when he walked alone, walking the walk of the living dead. His platoon was gone, and so he just kept walking, all the way back to base camp. When they sent him home to Lame Deer, he found himself still walking down that hill, pondering, "Why them and not me?—why me at all?"

Around the table the darkness was suddenly darker, each of us fully aware that we could not peer into the abyss Vernon had seen.

For in that place he saw all truths as lies save the nothingness on the other side of death, the nothingness at the bottom of the hill. And from that place a decision must be made—whether to live on in spite of it all, whether or not life is even possible in the absence of blind hopes and dreams.

Henry stood and placed a firm, tender hand on Vernon's shoulder. "You have the medicine and the powers. Your great great-grandfather was Ice. That's why the bullets couldn't touch you. You have that power."

But there was uncertainty. Vernon reached up and touched Henry's hand in polite acquiescence. Henry's speech was slurred and he was wobbling, his hand finding as much support from Vernon's shoulder as it had tried to give. His head bobbed as he teetered at the edge of passing out, and Vernon told him gently to sit down.

The darkness gave in a little to the first hints of dawn, and I looked at Henry and was frightened. I was suddenly convinced that it was he, not Vernon, who had made the decision about whether to live life anyway, and it was not in the affirmative.

I remained immobile at table's edge after Irene told Henry to go to bed and Tom found his way to the couch. And I lingered after she told Vernon to come to the kitchen and have some food. She put some dried meat in a pot to boil and began a muted Cheyenne monologue as she and Vernon stared out the back window into the Lame Deer dawn, and he echoed her words with sounds of comfort. And when the pot bubbled, she stopped talking and looked at me and said after a long silent look, "No, Jerry, this is not for you— this is Cheyenne food."

I went to bed. The heaviness of the night at last pulled me toward sleep, while images of the Bone Ranch and the trapped deer and Vernon's walk tossed and turned in my mind and folded themselves into a photograph of Ira Hayes I'd seen on the front page of the *Great Falls Tribune* when I was a child. There was no article, just a brief obituary under the photograph.

Ira was a Pima Indian who had been among those famous flag-raisers on Iwo Jima. He got the Congressional Medal of Honor for his efforts in the war, but the hero was still an Indian who couldn't vote in Arizona and couldn't find his way back to any home. Hayes died of alcoholism. The newspaper photo showed him all swollen from cirrhosis, drunk, holding the famous flag photo against his chest so the photographer could get a good shot of it. They found his body in an alley. The medal was still in his pocket. It had no doubt bought him a lot of drinks.

Like Ira, Vernon came home and was twice a stranger: once to the tribe, once again to the country he'd served. And it was little comfort for him to know that the white soldiers at last felt some of his exile when they came home to the ridicule of their peers.

I could hear Irene speaking steadily, the rhythm finally silencing the voices in my head as she talked Vernon into the sunrise and I fell asleep. Later, when Tom and Henry and I emerged to greet her, our hangovers, and the midday sun, Vernon was gone.

And then there was the day when we had to go out and find the Bone Ranch again, to probe its mysteries once more. We went despite Henry's resistance. But when we arrived, it was Tom and I who were spooked, because our mythical Bone Ranch was no more—just a black circle of scorched earth. Nothing remained, not even the pile of catsup bottles. The tomb of the deer had been swallowed by the earth; the spot where it had been was smooth and unmarked.

The surgical cauterization of our place of mystery seemed to confirm our darkest projections about its story, a story we were then sure had been known to those who came and burned the place to the ground—ground now utterly devoid of bones. We looked at Henry. He pleaded ignorance, but an air of satisfaction about him indicated well-guarded knowledge regarding the demise of the Bone Ranch.

And so we relegated it to our library of tales, catalogued it as a prelude to an evening of ghost stories, and then moved on to the day when the late afternoon found us wandering through waist-high grass at a ranch where a bell hung without its clapper high above the overgrown yard. The grasses laced in and around and through wrought-iron yard furniture and rosebushes once meticulously maintained by a rancher's wife who must have rung that enormous bronze bell each day for the noon meal. The grass snuggled around the feed troughs, the sagging barn eaves, and the sheds and all but hid the steps up to the front porch whose balustrades once contained evening talk over lemonade—talk we could almost hear as we knocked gently on the loosely latched front door.

Amid the silence of no reply a porch chair rocked slightly. Henry knocked again and then pushed the door open. I stepped into a parlor covered with doilies and photographs and then peered into a kitchen that sported a hand pump in the sink flanked by shelves well stocked with canned goods. On the table a plate reflected the memories of someone's breakfast. The thin afternoon light was comforting, and the chairs and table beckoned, but decorum pushed me back toward the door. Yet I had to pause in the parlor to glance at wedding pictures in cardboard oval frames and could not help but lightly touch the soft leather cover of the enormous Good Book stationed at the corner of the knotty pine armoire, and I held my breath under the steady tick of the Chelsea clock on the shelf and smiled as it struck the quarter hour.

Outside and away from the porch it was easy to imagine the hum of the place in its prime and that long pure tone from the bell. And then Henry appeared on the porch, descended the steps with great silence, and spoke with a hush.

"He's in there, sleeping in his little bed back of the kitchen. I thought he was dead, but he's just asleep. I've known him since I was a little kid. He's a good old man. His wife died a few years ago. His kids don't live around here anymore, so I come see him once in awhile, maybe take him to Colstrip. We don't talk much—he's real deaf now."

And there was the day whose afternoon heat restrained us on Henry's front porch, where we watched the heat waves wiggle upward from the road and sipped beer from cans disguised with plastic 7-Up sleeves. On that day the monotonous grind of nothing to do which is the relentless truth of Lame Deer day to day finally found us and presented us with an ennui beyond the scope of Baudelaire: the singular boredom resigned to despair that lives at the heart of any and every ghetto, the place where the human psyche can no longer delete or reframe the raw offensive actuality of every minute aspect of the environment. It is a world where everything living or dead is microscopically objectified, each thing a static particle within a Newtonian universe where all the clocks have stopped.

In a front yard across the street an abandoned car's slow oxidation proceeded almost visibly; its owner had adapted to its invisible mechanical decline without ever attempting a rescue. The rotting foundation of the house in that yard would proceed with or without the junk boards scabbed onto its hollow timbers. The broken window would remain broken, and someone would stuff it with rags and cover it again with plastic garbage bags when the weather turned bad. The paint inside and out would continue to peel, and the singular vagabond leak in the roof would breed with itself and task the family supply of pots when it rained. This was a place where entropy ruled, its relentless progression to disorder proceeding at its own ponderous pace with us at its center—stark, stoic, immobile.

We got drunk. Our blurred eyes synchronized with the heat waves, and we floated in the heat trance and didn't notice the first wisps of smoke rising above the crest of the hill until focus finally arrived with the bloody brown cloud of range fire that vaulted fifty feet above the horizon. And then we stood and fetched fresh cold ones and lined up along the porch rail to cheer the Forest Service boraid (fire retardant) bombers as they buzzed Henry's house and skimmed the top of the hill on their way to the fire. And we cheered each time we felt the concussion and saw the pink clouds rise and rise again until the smoke finally thinned and we settled back into the twilight and the night where darkness could camouflage our utterly conspicuous consumption of the preferred antidote to Lame Deer ennui. And we were grateful.

At last, in our gratitude, we offered our oblations to the gods of alcohol at the foot of the aluminum pyramid we'd constructed on the dining table in their honor and begged them to give us a cool morning for our hangovers. And our blissful, reverent mockery made it easy to cajole the sudden appearance of an unknown Tall Bull in Henry's clothing who said "Fuck that!—let's go to Jimtown and get some more beer!" We warned of the cops and giggled and put him to bed without a first or a second thought.

And there was the day when Henry guided us through the hottest of hot Montana afternoons along the back roads north of Colstrip. The allure of forgotten homestead dreams was fading as a certain dull redundancy crept into the subject matter. Most of the places we found were too far gone to suggest anything more than demolition. Yet we pressed on, the mystery of the Bone Ranch still fresh in our memories. And our spirits were heightened by a new member in our expeditionary team, Dick Littlebear.

When Tom was still in residence on the reservation, Dick had returned to Busby with a college degree in English and the rough draft of a novel. He had solicited Tom's advice as he struggled through the cycles of manic depression that so often infect the birth of a first novel. Dick's book would be a double premier, for he would then be the first Northern Cheyenne novelist.

Dick had taken the white man's road by going to college and pursuing literature and had found there the seeds for his own brand of Red Power. He had learned that in the white man's world, few were feared more than great writers; he believed, therefore, that a great Cheyenne writer might be the white man's worst nightmare. For beneath his typical Cheyenne modesty and sense of humor there was rage, the same rage suppressed by most Cheyenne men, especially Henry. But Dick's was a fury trying desperately to find form, lest it devour him from within as it had so many of his generation. He was a poet in the rough—raw, caustic, in love with the double entendre—and could really drink a lot of beer. He fit right in.

Certainly, beer was in the back of all our minds as the midafternoon temperature passed the 100-degree mark and taxed our collective patience. But Henry was determined to find a good picture for me, and when the road arched above a broad basin he stared into the distance and said, "Stop the car!"

A facsimile of the Dakota Badlands spread out beyond us, the valley finally butting up against a wall of sandstone pillars, small buttes, and box canyons. Near the center, two sandstone monoliths towered above it all, maybe two hundred feet above the valley floor. They were the objects of Henry's interest. "There's an eagle's nest on top of the big one!" he said, and we all stared through the heat waves and tried to sort reality from mirage. "You should get a picture. I'll bet they're nesting now."

I looked at him and then at the landscape. I saw nothing but a long hot walk in front of me but was not willing to argue. Tom and Dick just stared into the vastness and left the decision to me. I got out of the car, loaded thirty pounds of equipment on my back, and strode off into the furnace. After all, the sighting was made by the man who could shoot a deer in the eye at fifty yards in the dark with a 22-caliber rifle. And as I walked and peered through the vibrating heat waves, I was sure I saw the eagles and their nest.

But the farther I walked, the more distant the pillars seemed. When I looked back, the size of the Volvo fit the perspective well enough, but when I turned toward them again, those pillars had definitely moved farther away. And I could no longer see the nest.

On the high plains, when the temperature passes 100 degrees, the air progressively approaches solidity. When it reaches 110 and beyond, the atmosphere becomes a thermal straitjacket that inhibits your movements like those dreams wherein you try to flee from evil incarnate on legs of lead. About halfway to the pillars, I hit that wall of heat and stalled.

I put the camera bag down, wiped the sweat from my eyes, and let the landscape redistribute itself. At last Euclid won out and I saw the pillars as they really were: not quite so tall, less than dramatic, the eagle's nest merely the twisted skeleton of a long-dead jack pine. I felt the heat burn into my lungs as I took a deep breath and looked back at the car. It was empty and my companions were nowhere to be seen. And then I felt the humiliation that was sure to come. I'd been had, and there was little to do but walk back and face it.

I knew I was going to be the brunt of whatever practicality their joke would inspire, and my anticipation of their delight reminded me of another humiliation I'd recently received, from Philip Whiteman's children. I could feel the heat rising up through the soles of my shoes and the sun was boring into my skull. I took my time and walked slowly and remembered the day that Tom and I went to Philip's house to hear him sing.

Philip Whiteman was, by consensus, the best of the Cheyenne singers. He was a dedicated artist who could be heard practicing day or night; passersby often heard his songs emanating from the outhouse, where the acoustics suited him and he could beat out the rhythm of the song of the day on its walls. He had much to prepare because from early spring until late fall he followed the powwow circuit from Canada to Oklahoma, singing and collecting songs with his cassette recorder. He was riding the crest of the new Pan-Indian movement in which participants from all tribes were exchanging music, stories, and traditional practices and generating a real cultural resurgence among indigenous peoples across North America.

I'd had classical training as a musician and composer, but I wanted to broaden my experience by learning Cheyenne music and decided that the best way was to learn to sing it. When I asked Philip to teach me, he got out his drum, a huge bass salvaged from some school's marching band, and proceeded to sing, as he said, "a easy song." His four children gathered around us, grinned and rocked with the beat, and curiously awaited my first attempt.

"A easy song" rose above the drum beat with a melismatic intricacy comparable only to Islamic chant or East Indian raga, the root melody buried inside the improvisation. My classical training was suddenly useless, my ear tuned to another precision. I was lost but undaunted, and so when Philip invited me to try, I launched forth with gusto.

Whatever my throat released at that moment, it bore little resemblance to what he'd demonstrated. Philip stopped drumming instantly, utterly confounded by what he was hearing. His children, convulsed with laughter, lost their balance and rolled on the floor with tears streaming until they just lay there gasping for breath. Tom observed later that he'd been unaware until that moment that humans were capable of such sounds, but the death wails of certain mammals came to mind as relevant comparisons. For Philip Whiteman's children, however, I provided the funniest exhibition they'd ever seen, and they begged for more. Although clearly amused as well, he gently reminded them of their manners and banished them to the kitchen, where they furtively peeked around the door jamb as the lesson proceeded.

I listened again and tried again but with little improvement. Philip suggested he make a tape so I could practice at home—a strategy sure to preserve his sanity and whatever was left of my dignity but greatly disappointing for the peeking children. As the weeks progressed, however, they became my groupies, counting on my continued failures to fill their little lives with high comedy. The lessons stopped when Philip took off for his annual tour of powwows, but my groupies were loyal and undaunted. Whenever they saw me in Lame Deer, they rushed to my side pleading, "Sing for us again! Sing for us again!" Then they followed me, chanting, attracting other children until there was a horde of them, all begging for my musical humiliation. I don't know what Philip really thought, but I'm sure he was grateful when I finally stopped appearing for lessons and thereby removed a serious threat to Pan-Indian music.

When I got to the car, there was no sound. The windows were rolled up, the doors locked. Whatever the ruse, I wasn't playing. I sat on my camera box in the shade of the car and prayed for one of the occasional breezes that skitter a few inches above the ground on hot afternoons, always tantalizing, marginally cooling.

And then it began, that same singsong chanting tone I'd learned to fear from Philip Whiteman's children, transposed into Dick Littlebear's octave, now bleating from every direction: "Eagle Fingers, Eagle Fingers!! Help us! Help us! We're so thirsty—help us, Eagle Fingers! Use your light-box medicine to make us some beer! We thirst, Eagle Fingers! Help us!"

When they appeared at last, Henry covered his laughter with his hand; Tom repeatedly denied complicity; and Dick confessed. "I bet Henry five bucks you would walk all the way out there before you figured it out, but you didn't, so I decided you should have a Cheyenne nickname. Jerry Eaglechaser came to mind, but Henry thinks Eaglefingers suits you better. Anyway, now I'm broke. That was my last five bucks, and since we gave you a name, you could buy us some beer, huh? Take pity on a poor Indian?"

There was little choice. Colstrip was just over the hill, and unlike the eagle's nest the bar was *there*. As for my new name, the sarcasm in Dick's voice and the look on Henry's face belied the actuality of "Eaglefingers." I was sure it was an expurgated version of a pornographic nominalization I would rather not know. My suspicion was confirmed by their furtive laughter while they called me Eaglefingers all the way to Colstrip and discovered aerie after aerie hidden within the general mirage and assured me each time that there really were eagles out there.

And then there came the day when I knew things were going to get worse for Henry and that I was caught within a progression of events I could neither control nor divert. I knew all that and more when I found myself standing on the sidewalk on the Southside of Billings in front of the Red Rose Tavern. I stood there and caught my breath and let that epiphany take root in me. When it did, I looked up and down the street and knew this was exactly where I did not want to be.

I looked up and down the street and then up at the clapboard facade of the bar where a painted rose leached dirty pink into the cracked wood, the antique lettering barely separated from knots and whorls. In my head I could hear Henry's plea, "You can do it, Jerry, they won't recognize you!" Maybe so, I thought, but I did recognize where I was. I looked across the street at the rail crossing and felt a childhood fear rush up my spine and remembered another day long before this one when my childhood self, hungry for danger, sneaked out along the tracks on the south side of Great Falls and peeked inside the open door of the Caboose Bar until the mean-looking drunk came out and threatened to kick my ass. And I remembered walking along Central Avenue with my mom and nearly tripping over the man who was sprawled on the pavement, passed out, hugging his wine bottle while everyone just kept walking, and when I stopped to stare she pulled me away. I heard Henry's voice again: "C'mon, Jerry!—I gotta get that tape recorder back!"

I was on the other Montana Indian reservation, the one nobody talks about except city councilmen just before elections, or urban planners who stare across the tracks and dream of future developments. This was the Indian reservation open to all tribes, mixed-blood or full, and drinking was allowed here. I heard Henry's voice in my head again and saw Irene's face there too. "Their names are José and Blackie. It's a rough place, but if you go in the afternoon it's okay. José and Blackie are there in the afternoon. It's only been a few days—maybe they haven't fenced the tape recorder yet."

I looked up and down the street again. This was the street they'd described. I saw Irene's worried face in my mind's eye again as I tried to guess where her daughter had lived. Irene said it was near the Red Rose. There were apartments above most of the stores, and a lot of run-down houses and shacks beyond the tracks. "We had to get her out of there," Irene said. "I know he was beating her. He was no good, that one!" The door swung open and dislodged a round swollen figure that paused in front of me and asked, "Help a poor Indian?" and pressed against me as I pushed past him into the Red Rose.

Inside, I stepped away from the door but kept my back against the wall. "Blackie is the bartender. He's a Mexican. He has big tattoos on his arms." Henry was right. This was the place and that was Blackie behind the bar. Beneath it, large galvanized washtubs were filled with ice and beer cans. One tap graced the center of the bar. Blackie worked the tubs and tap without ever looking at his hands. His narrow eyes scanned the room incessantly, watching for the first signs of the worst, which was sure to happen.

He saw me right away and suddenly all the jokes Henry and Tom and I made about the mythical "Blackie" and "José" from some B-rated film noir weren't funny anymore. I knew I should leave right then and forget it. But Irene's voice welled up inside me and pushed me toward the bar. "She called us up—she was crying. It's lucky Henry was at the store when she called the pay phone there. He had to keep going inside to get more quarters when she ran out of money for the call. I wish we had a phone at home. She said he was on a bender, her husband, for three days! She wanted Henry to come get her. Henry ran home and we took off. He forgot the tape recorder was in the back seat. Somebody stole it while we were looking for her." And then I was on a bar stool looking at the foam atop my fifteen-cent beer, trying not to look at Blackie, who eyed me suspiciously while he wiped glasses and set up the bar.

And then, I froze amid a sudden surge of warmth in my groin. The hottest hand I have ever felt was pressed firmly into my crotch and furtively kneaded my inner thigh. As I turned my head quickly to discover its owner, her words fell on me like stale molasses: "Wanna buy me a beer, honey? We could have some fun." Beneath empty, cavernous eyes her skin hung from her cheekbones like burnt parchment. The flowers on her faded sun dress had nearly lost their outlines, as had the withered body that sagged beneath them.

She put her free arm around my shoulders and drew me to her, lust flashing weakly at the edges of her suddenly darker eyes. Her half-open mouth lurched toward mine and released a lover's gasp laced with tobacco and sour mash. The kiss missed its mark, but her chin found my shoulder. I felt her damp gray hair press into my neck while she tightened her grip on my thigh.

When the schooner I'd ordered for her hit the bar, she released me like a bad habit. She needed both hands. While she inhaled the cool release, Blackie looked sideways at her and then straight at me while he clucked his tongue and sneered "Half-breeds!"

I downed my beer, slid off the stool, and sought refuge at the other end of the bar. My temptress looked at me with eyes full of amnesia, just once, over the shoulder of the man who'd taken my place. I asked myself, "Why are you here?" and then remembered.

I remembered Henry's face as he sat on the couch with John Woodenlegs after he told John the tape recorder had been stolen. His face was ashen, and there was a tremor in his hand as he took furtive sips from a large glass of water and looked straight ahead while John and Tom considered what to do. The budget for the writing project could not afford another tape recorder. It was a Uher field recorder; a new one cost $350. John was stoic, but his anger was almost tangible in every corner of the room. I knew that everything unspoken between them would come back to plague Henry; there were so many kinds of failure there just waiting to accuse him. And I knew that as angry as John was, he would try to help Henry and would encourage Henry to come to a prayer meeting. And I knew Henry wouldn't go. All the condemnation we'd heard at Bessie Elkshoulder's cabin on that hot afternoon a year ago would find its way back to Henry and John again. Maybe it already had. Maybe that was why Henry had gone to the Red Rose. Maybe . . .

I tried to stay focused. I didn't want to go where those thoughts were taking me. I looked down the bar. Where my lady of the afternoon had been now sat a very white, doughy white man with dyed black hair cut in a flat top with wings and a ducktail. His small blue eyes were even smaller behind black-framed 1950s-style collegiate glasses. José. "He always wears those glasses and a blue Hawaiian shirt with gardenias on it," Henry said. "When you see him, tell him you like to go to powwows and you're looking for a used tape recorder. Say you heard there was somebody down there who had a good one, a field recorder."

I said my lines while José fiddled with his gold pinkie ring and then held a cigarette by its filter with his teeth while he lit it and then exhaled in my direction when I finished. He told me to try a pawnshop and then moved to the opposite end of the bar, where Blackie was waiting. They both looked sideways at me while I finished my beer and left.

Outside, the round man had appointed himself doorman and was seated on the sidewalk with a bottle of Thunderbird. He asked me again, and I gave him a dollar bill. He said "God bless you!" again and again as I moved slowly away—uncertain, briefly, as to exactly where I should go.

It was late in the afternoon, late in August, and the sun had dropped low, the rimrocks above the city suddenly gold. The windows of all the homes nestled against the rim began to shimmer in the sunset, and the sidewalk turned amber beneath my feet. Some Indian children played in the vacant lot across the street near the tracks, and farther down, in a small house at the head of a side street, a woman with a sleeping baby draped over her forearm leaned through the open door and called out—I thought to the ones playing in the lot, but they didn't respond. She called again and then disappeared within.

I wondered why all the bad bars and tough neighborhoods were always on the south side in Montana towns. I paused at the corner and for a second thought I might see Henry coming down from 1st Avenue, across the tracks. I imagined explaining what happened and apologizing for failing my mission.

I could see the car up ahead near the next rail crossing, where Tom was waiting, the engine running. He saw me and gave the horn a short one, but I hesitated. I looked up at the expensive homes on the rim again. Up there they had a panoramic view of Billings and the rich sprawl of the Yellowstone basin, but they couldn't see this street or me or the Red Rose Tavern or the round man sitting on the sidewalk. Nor could they see those who came from Lame Deer or Crow Agency or Pine Ridge, the ones who came looking for a better life, trying for a way out—maybe to try Eastern Montana College. Up there on the rim, the people in those big houses could see the college, but they couldn't see the ones who came here to the south side, just to lose themselves.

I stood on that sidewalk and knew this was where Henry came sometimes to continue a bender, to lose himself in it. And I knew that he was going to lose himself for all time on the south side of somewhere, just as surely as I knew I had to go back to Lame Deer and see him one more time. The windows of the fancy houses along the rimrocks were brilliant red orange. I turned and walked to the car.

And then there came the day when I journeyed to Lame Deer alone. Tom had been there for a week. He and Henry were trying to salvage whatever material had been collected before the tape recorder was stolen. I was more and more uneasy the closer I got to Lame Deer. I knew how desperate Henry had felt about the theft, and my forebodings had increased since I'd failed my rescue mission at the Red Rose. So when I pulled up in front of the house I wasn't surprised to see that they had, as Henry said when he marked the genesis of any bender, "got started."

The door was open and I could see Irene inside. Henry and Tom were on the porch, their "cool ones" masquerading in 7-Up sleeves. Henry called out, "Hey Eaglefingers!" and for a long moment I hesitated. But in spite of a sudden urge to pull away and drive back to Missoula, I got out of the car.

They were glad to see me, and I was also glad to see Dick Littlebear, who had come over from Busby specifically to greet "Eaglefingers." Irene's daughter Janet had arrived, safely disconnected from her husband in Billings. Her baby wasn't there, and I didn't ask. Janet had "got started" too, and of course there was a case of beer on the table. It was hot and they were waiting for me so we could all go up to the Ashland Divide for a picnic.

We feasted up there in the pines until the long summer twilight brought cool air, full bellies, and more beer. And then, with the darkness, came the inevitable release of all that is repressed and can be released only by alcohol. The resentments and failed expectations Irene and Janet shared as mother and daughter bubbled to the surface, with Henry somewhere left of center. Soon enough, tempers rose and invective accelerated. Henry had brought his .22 for target practice, and when Janet hurled a particularly virulent insult his way, Dick took the rifle and hid it in Tom's car. When she told me in Cheyenne, and Dick translated, that my face reminded her of the stains in her ex-husband's shorts, Tom tried to placate everyone by suggesting we all go back to the house for coffee. But Dick found Janet's "stained shorts" simile funny and laughed hard enough to get Irene laughing, and then we all discovered that violence was impossible when we were laughing—at least for a while.

The laughter died quickly in the sudden darkness, and in the night chill Irene and Henry peeled away the layers of resentment between them. Tom, once again, invoked calm and rationality, but they were having none of it. She accused Henry of sleeping around; he charged that she was frigid, and then the fight required their native tongue for proper syntax. Janet hurled insults at both of them and then asked Tom to take her to Busby, where she'd stay with a girlfriend. Dick said he'd go with them and suggested I drive Henry and Irene home in Henry's car. Henry protested, but when he couldn't find the door handle and Irene correctly identified him as too drunk to drive, he gave me the key. It, of course, had no function beyond activating the electrical system—the ignition switch had died years earlier. It was a Cheyenne car.

Tom drove away like a bandit in flight, while Henry informed me that he really should drive because I didn't know how to start his "weekend special." Irene cut him off: "It's easy, Jerry, just turn the lights on and then touch those two wires together—the ones under the dash by the steering column." And then she and Henry resumed their struggle, which now included sideways shoving on the front seat, while I fumbled in the dark for the wires.

The lights went on dimly, and then I found the wires, made contact, and jumped away from the spray of sparks that covered my legs as the engine turned once and died. I almost yielded when Henry said, "See, he can't do it—I should drive." Irene pushed him hard and said something that was obviously foul, and he pushed her back. I had no choice. I pumped the gas, made contact again, and as the sparks illuminated their angry faces, the engine unbelievably started. I revved it and headed for the main road.

Sparks erupted spasmodically from beneath the dashboard all the way down into Lame Deer, and for each of those endless miles, Henry and Irene continued their private war. They pushed and shoved and cursed each other while the car lurched and rocked, sparked and flashed, and occasionally backfired. Somehow it got us home before its anemic alternator gave its spirit to the night. I let the car coast into the front yard to seek and find its final resting place. Then, perhaps out of respect for the dead, Henry and Irene finally stopped fighting.

"Oh look, Henry—Jerry's worried about us fighting. It's all right, Jerry, this is just the way we fight, isn't it, Henry." He mumbled something and put his arm around my shoulders and squeezed a little. "How do you like my car?" He didn't wait for an answer but turned to help Irene hobble into the house.

I stood in the front yard and tried to regain my composure. I'd left the car lights on, but rather than rescue them, I deferred to the gods of General Motors and watched the dim glow fade into nothingness before I went inside.

Next morning the plains heat arrived with a vengeance. By ten o'clock it was 80 degrees. Tom had returned in the night and was the last to come to the dining table and face its centerpiece—

another case of beer. Henry was on his third cold one by the time Irene served breakfast, and by noon the parade of visitors had begun, all drawn by the pheromones released from that first case of beer. It was replaced again and again, of course, with the ebb and flow of guests who brought food as well and conversation and laughter. Among those who stayed the day were Mary Fisher and her son Terry, and Mary Teeth and her daughter Erlyce.

It was Mary Teeth who insisted, after her enormous wit and size had filled an entire roll of film, that I make portraits of the children. They sat for me easily—Terry, an open, intelligent boy, and Erlyce, whose retardation permitted her only marginal awareness of what I was doing. They were my last portrait subjects on the reservation. In the flat open light of Henry's front porch I saw them as two sides of the same innocence, one deeply inward, the other reaching out. They shared a smile that knew neither enlightenment nor dissolution. I pushed the limits of exposure, trying to capture that dual aspect of their presence—each an entrance and an exit, a beginning and an ending.

When I stepped back into the house, Mary Fisher was pleading her case to Irene, who had already offered her a place to stay. But Mary needed to explain. She did have money, really, but she'd left it with the bartender in Ashland so her husband wouldn't get it. He'd abandoned her there when the bar closed at two in the morning. She and Terry had hitched rides into Lame Deer. If she could get that money, she'd be on her way to Forsyth. She had relatives there. She would divorce him.

And then, as if endowed with psychic radar, she looked at Tom and me—and so did Irene. Of course we would take her to Ashland and get the money. We piled into Tom's car and headed up the divide. While Mary continued her nonstop apology, I remembered my first visit to Ashland's premier saloon.

As a would-be stylish cowboy saloon, the Ashland Bar was a work in progress. Its newly improved knotty pine and oak appointments, stuffed elk and moose heads, and a massive set of Texas longhorns over the bar failed, however, to attract clientele much above the social strata of the south side of Billings. It was a dive, albeit a pretty one, pretending to be more subtle than the archetype. Unlike the Red Rose, however, where time had for all purposes stopped, the Ashland Bar revealed its desolate qualities incrementally with the passage of time—the hour before closing reserved for the utterly lost, who had to be pried from the altar of oblivion and forced out onto the banks of the Tongue River.

Indeed, one's ability to hold one's liquor could be and was noted by the time of day. Expertise and character were morally equivalent, and the rubric was applied within a democracy where equality is that which does not exist among equals. Being a drunk cowboy at two in the afternoon was not only bad taste; it meant that the cowboy was very close to the edge of the pit reserved for the red man and needed help. By contrast, a drunk Indian at two in the afternoon was in violation of the schedule and needed to be thrown out. In sum, the Indian was a degenerate, whereas the cowboy merely had a drinking problem.

But at closing time, the darker purpose beneath the time warp finally revealed itself. At 2:00 A.M. any night and especially on weekends, cowboy and Indian reenacted their Hollywood history of violence, betrayal, and murder as they'd seen it done by Republic Pictures at the Rialto in Forsyth. And when the battles were over, stitches taken, and the maimed or dead hauled away, that history was confirmed. The cowboy, down on his luck, was exonerated. The Indian was—well—an Indian who couldn't hold his liquor and should stay on the reservation where he belonged.

The arbiter, timekeeper, and stage manager for this theater of the absurd was the bartender, and at the Ashland Bar he affirmed another historical precedent: the traditional one of the whiskey trader who hated Indians but loved their money more. He assuaged the rich ranchers who came in for an afternoon pick-me-up by throwing out the Indians who were too far gone too early. And then, as the schedule moved on and evened out the alcoholic demography, he let them in again.

As we left Lame Deer and started up the Ashland Divide, Mary Fisher gave us all the dirt on the bartender she knew. It was a grim picture of a sneak who stole money from drunk Indians at closing time after they were all passed out or just too drunk to care. She said this bartender let Indians run tabs against their allotment checks and then cheated them by saying they owed more than they really did. She hoped he remembered that he was keeping her money for her behind the bar. She said he put it in an envelope with her name on it.

It was two-thirty in the afternoon when we pulled up in front of the bar. We stepped inside and the room got very quiet. I knew we were in the wrong place at the wrong time.

A half-dozen cowboys in white shirts, white straw hats, and sunglasses achieved a new rigidity in the silence. An equal number of Indians, teetering at the limits of consumption for the proscribed hour, were uninterested. The bartender moved toward us, increasing the distance between himself and the cowboys, who remained immobile but gave us the long stare.

At the bar, only he and I faced each other. Even as Mary reminded him of the night before, he refused to look at her. And even as his denials rose beneath her pleas for recognition, his eyes remained fixed on mine, waiting to exchange the tacit look of complicity with me that would acknowledge the weariness of the maligned public servant who must put up with the whines of the indolent. But when they did not receive that confirmation of shared reality, those eyes reasserted themselves in an instant and redefined me as one of "them."

And with that, I was given a close look into the face and the anatomy of hatred: the skin suddenly taut around the jawbone, the eyes narrowed slightly and the skin blanched around them, the lips thinner, the tongue working itself behind clenched teeth as if preparing to spit, the rest of the body tense with readiness, supporting the cause, ready to lean hard into confrontation.

His was a hatred whose dual purpose was to eradicate all that he hated and to take pleasure in the violence of doing it. I looked into his face and felt a hopeless sickness in my gut. I looked into his face and saw nothing but a wasteland where reason and compassion had died an unredeemable death. I looked into his face and felt my despair turn to rage. I wanted to hit him.

Mary was choking on her tears, stuttering, trying to refute the lie. "Lady, I told ya, I ain't never seen you before in my life and I ain't got no God-damned envelope!" The lie sent a wave of righteousness up my spine. But before I could respond, a weathered female whiskey voice came from behind us and slurred something in Cheyenne at Mary, who quickly reached across me and grabbed that voice's throat with both hands.

The voice continued to gag out insults while its owner tried to kick and slap herself loose. Mary let go and delivered an uppercut that launched the woman into the air, where the long arc of her flight assisted the fall of her baggy pants, which found her ankles precisely as she hit the wall. She was up in a second, spitting blood and Algonquian profanity, stumbling, her hands floundering between gesture and her lost trousers.

I grabbed Mary's arm and pulled her toward the door. Tom pushed both of us from behind, sandwiching her between us while a wave of white hats rose up, and he kept shouting "Out!! Out!!" like a plugged bugle. I looked over my shoulder and saw the bartender reach down behind the bar as we squeezed out the door.

It swung freely behind us and no one followed, but we were too full of adrenaline to notice. By the time we reached the car our disorderly retreat had achieved Chaplinesque proportions. The doors were still swinging as the Volvo fishtailed its way to the blacktop and left a good five minutes' worth of dust to settle in front of the Ashland Bar. "That Crow bitch called me a whore!"

By the time we reached the coolness at the crest of the divide, Mary's weeping had settled into the relentless subterranean rhythm of despair. I reached over the seat back and offered her my handkerchief. Tears dropped slowly from her nose and chin to her half-exposed breast while her trembling fingers failed again and again to reassemble her torn blouse and modesty. She did not look at me as she took the handkerchief but briefly pressed the back of my hand into the place where her tears had fallen. I withdrew it quickly and turned and blinked through the glare of sunlight on the windshield.

Back at the house, Mary disappeared into the spare room that Irene had made into a bedroom for her and the boy. The rest of us berated the bartender, whose corruption increased by the minute. All the while, new faces came and went, leaving the well at the center of the table ever replenished. Women moved in and out of the spare room, taking clothing and food and, I supposed, comfort to Mary. And then it seemed that everyone had left her alone. Her son was out on the porch with Henry when an enormous Cheyenne man emerged from her room, one I'd somehow missed. He scanned the company briefly, tucked in his shirt, fastened his trousers and belt, and left. Moments later, Mary came out with suitcase in hand and asked Tom for a ride into Lame Deer; she said she had to meet somebody there for a ride to Forsyth. She thanked Irene and went out on the porch. Tom lingered over his beer before he followed. As he stepped out the door, Irene said, "Tom—tell her she better watch out for her husband now." He nodded, and she did her best to suppress a laugh.

After Mary left, the visitation slowed, and we moved inside to escape the heat on the porch. Irene had started to fry some chicken, and Henry was dozing on the couch. I felt a little relieved and hoped the party would wind down. Tom and I sat at the table with a young white guy who said he was an anthropologist doing field-work at Crow Agency.

He had lots of questions for Tom, and eventually their talk settled around the Sun Dance. Henry heard it, got up from the couch, and joined us after opening yet another cool one.

The white guy was delighted and had even more questions for Henry about the Sun Dance and the Crows. Clearly, he didn't understand that Cheyennes rarely had anything good to say about Crows, especially about their Sun Dance. Tom did his best to run interference, but when the white guy said he was going to attend the Crow ceremony, it was too much for Henry.

He vaulted out of his chair and lunged into the young man's face: "Crow Sun Dance is shit!" The young man's pale face found an even paler shade, and he froze; Henry was going to hurt him and he knew it. Tom and I pushed between them while the young man apologized and made a quick exit. But the storm had just begun.

After dinner the beer flowed on, and Henry just wouldn't let it go. The Crows let white people watch the Sun Dance and that was sacrilege. And the sacrilege was double because the young anthropologist was going to watch anyway, even though he knew it was embarrassing. Henry blamed Hyemeyohsts Storm's book *Seven Arrows* for encouraging white people to participate in Indian sacred ceremonies and for misrepresenting Cheyenne religion: "He said in that book that the Sun Dance priest sleeps with his own mother!"

And then he delivered an untranslatable yet unmistakable poem of rage and despair. It came in short and long bursts of Cheyenne and English, mixed and matched within the relentless rhythm of condemnation. Henry was giving voice and testimony for every injustice and sin perpetrated against his people, and he would not be silenced.

I listened to it all come out of him and watched his body and personality distort. I saw him twist within the alcoholic fog like a snared cougar. He was trapped. Somewhere at some time in his history he'd taken "that drink" that is one too many, the one that tipped the balance. It may have been the first or the hundredth, it didn't matter, because at last he'd found a way to numb out the pain, the sense of failure, the self-loathing, the death of God. And with every drink after "that drink," he steadily created another need, the one known by every addict, which makes no distinctions of race, creed, or ethnicity, nor does it care any longer about the metaphor of the Sun Dance. For within that need nothing remains but the fractured metaphor of the addict who falls through the looking-glass into the land where the Bread-and-Butter-Fly lives on beer and hedgehogs are croquet balls and flamingos are mallets and the Queen of Hearts paints the roses red.

Relentlessly, all our attempts to calm, to redirect, to change the subject failed until at last he was on his feet, where the incoherent litany found new volume and rhythm until Irene cut him off. Her rebuke stopped him only for a minute. He nullified it with histori-cal potency: "My great-grandfather was Ice!" And then he wobbled and leaned close to my face and hissed it at me directly: "Jerry—my great-grandfather was Ice!"

I recoiled within the fetid smell of rotten hops that had risen out of him with his words and realized that what stood before me then had no name. What stood before me then was the personification of that which I'd felt beneath my fingertips, beneath the scars as I anointed his face with baby oil one gray winter morning. What stood before me then was all that remained after the alcohol had peeled away the layered artifice of his persona, the mask he so des-perately tried to maintain. What stood before me then was the per-sonification of his inexplicable need for identity and its equally in-explicable need for self-destruction.

What stood before us all had risen up out of some nameless wound inside him, and the transformation was complete. His form was distorted, eyes vacant, mouth set hard between rage and sorrow. His voice echoed the hollowness of the place whence it came, demanding death again and again as his hands tore open his shirt and he thrust his bare chest out to expose his heart: "Kill Me! Kill Me!"

Then Tom and Irene and I rose up and danced with him, a macabre push-and-pull. Like a Cocteau version of the Three Graces, we danced him away from the spare room where the guns were, away from the kitchen and the knives. We kept turning and dancing and turning until he leaned against the arm of the couch and waved us off and fell backward into unconsciousness.

We arranged his limp body on the couch and Irene covered him with a blanket. And then we sat within the dumb silence of the house and the darkness and tried in vain to fill either or both with clichés and platitudes until the silence won, and we relinquished ourselves to the night. I lay on the other side of the wall from his couch and listened to him breathe and replayed it all again and again in my mind. And again and again I saw his doppleganger standing before me crying out in rage and despair, "My great-grandfather was Ice!"

I too cried out, silently, in the dark at that ghost. I wanted an explanation from that ghost. I wanted to know why it had come to claim the life of the man in the next room, the man with whom it shared the breath of life, the man I'd grown to love.

I lay in the dark and listened to him breathe on the other side of the wall and measured the spaces between aspirations, fearful in the silences, grateful when each breath was taken. I lay there and listened, ready at every moment to rush into the living room and shake him into life again should he stop breathing altogether.

I lay inside that darkness and my own confusion, haunted by all the questions that would not be answered. "Why hadn't I seen this coming? Why did I drink with him when I knew better? Why didn't I say something? Why didn't I do something? Why can't I seem to find a way to help? Why can't I even determine what 'help' might be if I had the courage to act? Why don't I have that courage? What if there is nothing I or anyone else can do? What do I do about that? What will I do tomorrow?"

I lay in the dark and found no answers.

Much later, when his breathing at last found a rhythm, I found resignation. Whatever was required to save Henry from himself was beyond my capability. I did not even know how to try. I did know I would not come back, not without a way to help him. If I could not find a way to help him get well, I knew for certain I would not help him die.

The morning after came at last. I stepped through the fog of my insomnia into the dining room. Henry was chugging down his first cold one of the day when Tom emerged from his bed in Henry's study. I said goodbye to Henry and motioned to Tom to follow me outside.

We leaned against the side of my car with our backs to the house and lit cigarettes and tried to find some way to talk about anything. At last he managed a full sentence.

"Henry's just upset over the tape recorder. He'll be all right—really."

I took a long drag and didn't look at him.

"You know," I said, "I don't think so. Anyway, I can't do this anymore." He didn't speak. I waited and then flicked my cigarette into the road. "I don't think you should either."

He was quick to reply: "I'll be all right. We'll get the project finished—it'll be all right."

Tom stood on the porch as I pulled away. I looked back after I made the U-turn in front of the house and headed into Lame Deer, but he had already gone inside.

The road home from Lame Deer was long that day. All the imponderables from the night before haunted every mile, and no matter how I tallied it all, it just wouldn't sum. I had gone too far and was lost.

Tom returned to Missoula a week later after Tobie insisted he come home. He called and with deep need in his voice asked if we could get together. But something had grown hard inside me, and I didn't believe him. I didn't believe he was going to do anything new. I knew he was going to continue with Henry despite what anyone might say. He believed he could work it through. I knew that and put him off.

Over the next several weeks I put more distance between us. I hid behind my ongoing labor on the Marquis project and other work. I refused when he asked me to travel to Lame Deer with him. And I felt a different sort of distance and resignation as I watched Henry and Dick and Janet find their way to Tom's front porch later that summer, where the party continued. Occasionally I heard my name called from across the street—"Hey! Eaglefingers! we miss you!"—and eventually I did go across for a brief exchange of greetings. I said I couldn't stay.

Later that fall the state received its typical post-Thanksgiving blizzard. Tom fought it through eighteen hours of driving from Lame Deer to Missoula. Things had been deteriorating again at Henry's house, and the writing project was permanently stalled.

Tom hoped a change of venue would interrupt the bender, and so he brought Henry and Irene home with him.

The Volvo had barely come to rest on snow-clogged McLeod Avenue before Henry was out, across the street, and knocking at my door. Before I could speak, his arms were around me, the side of his face pressed hard against my chest. He was drunk and wobbly. He leaned his head back while still holding me tight, looked straight at me, and spoke. The words slurred, but as he said them the fog cleared from his eyes long enough for me to see him.

"We think the world of you—we think the world of you!" And then he pressed his face into my chest again, and we held each other amid the feathery wet snowfall and inhaled winter air laced with the smell of stale beer. I was suddenly fearful, but I didn't know it was the last time I would see him.

I followed him across the street, and we all sat in Tom's kitchen and tried to be gracious. Tom and I talked a bit for the first time since that night when we'd all danced with the ghost in Henry's living room. I excused myself after refusing a fresh cold one. The bender wasn't quite over yet.

That winter seemed incapable of finding springtime, and all through it I was haunted by a recurring dream. It was always the same, although its appearance was entirely unpredictable. Each time, I awakened violently, wrenched into consciousness, sweating, gasping for breath, sitting straight up in bed searching the predawn darkness for signs of familiarity. And each time, I at last fell back on the pillow and waited for the feelings of utter dread to dissolve while I searched the dream for relevance.

In the dream I am seated at the table in Grover's kitchen. Grover and I are alone and I feel awkward, even though I know I am his guest. It is night and all the windows are black walls. I know I'm in Grover's house, but I can't see the lights from Lame Deer outside. I can't see out at all. The single light bulb hanging from the ceiling is the only light on in the house, but its brightness is almost unbearable. I know I've been invited for dinner but I feel anxious, unwanted. Grover is standing in front of the stove with his back to me. There is no heat in the kitchen, no smells of cooking. And then he turns toward me with two metal plates in his hands. He isn't looking at me, but I know he is angry. I look down at my plate. I see four perfectly spherical pieces of earth, mud balls, about an inch in diameter. They look like clay but have that distinctive olive shade of peyote buttons. They are very moist looking, as if cast with dew. I look at Grover's plate; he has the same. I touch one—it is clay, and my finger leaves a small impression on the surface. I hesitate, looking at him. He says, "This is what we have." I'm confused. I know he's waiting for me to eat. He doesn't sit down but looks straight ahead, still holding his plate. He says it again, louder, as if defending against an imminent complaint. "This is what we have!" I don't want to insult him. I pick up one of the clay spheres. The cold, moist surface of the earth morsel just touches my tongue as I'm thrust into the darkness of my own bedroom, and I gasp for air.

The dream haunted me throughout most of the next year. Tom and Tobie left Missoula for a nine-month stay in Washington DC while she did research at the Smithsonian. I finished the first edition of three hundred prints from the Marquis collection and waited for spring and decent weather to make the delivery. Late March found me on the road to Lame Deer and a meeting that would bring us all together again—all but Henry.

We met at St. Labre Mission in Ashland. Tom had flown in from DC to help confirm the final edit on his *History of the Cheyenne People*. John Woodenlegs was deeply pleased, eager to get the book into the schools. Tom and I were glad to see each other. Geographic distance and time had softened things between us. When I asked, Tom said Henry and Irene were back east attending a friend's graduation from college.

John was delighted with everything the research association had accomplished. We pored over the Marquis photos, the history text, and the last of the storybooks Tom and Henry had produced. There was a real sense of accomplishment and the somewhat liberating realization that whatever our failures, we had survived. Yet I wished that Henry had been at that meeting to share the wealth.

Tom and I had lunch together before I left. He made small talk about Washington, and I brought him up to date on Missoula gossip. An awkward silence after lunch invited us to make excuses and seek forgiveness, but we let it pass. I asked if he'd heard from Henry recently. He had not but assured me Henry was doing better. And then I drove him back to St. Labre's and took off for Missoula.

As if for old time's sake, a spring blizzard slapped at the car all the way out of Lame Deer, and I plowed through the slush steadily, not stopping until I got to Bozeman. I sat in a truck stop and sipped coffee and watched the big sloppy snowflakes melt on the pavement. As each one fell and dissolved, it seemed to confirm and deny all the ways we can and cannot help each other.

Over the next year my dream about Grover persisted but with less frequency. Tom and Tobie returned to Missoula, and we found ways back to our friendship. And then spring came again, early, and with it the last appearance of my dream. It came the night before I got the phone call from Tom telling me that Henry was dead.

"Just thought you'd like to know," he said after giving me the confused details surrounding his death. "I'm going down for the funeral." He went on as if reading an obituary for the late night news: date, age, survivors, funeral schedule. I mumbled something and he hung up and I just stood there—lost in the wasteland of the dial tone.

7

The door was closing slowly, without hesitation. Our eyes were locked as we searched for a way to say the words. Then, with but two inches of visibility between us, she minutely nodded her head and her eyes drifted down as she turned away.

The latch clicked. It was such a small sound. I wondered if this was the way of all endings—neither whimper nor bang, just a slight tremor on the wider surface of things. We had been unable to say those last words, and so I let go of Irene Tall Bull silently, knowing that the sound of the door and the look in her eyes would be with me forever.

It was Saturday noon in Lame Deer and I had nothing to do. The business I had with John Woodenlegs would occur within the chronology of Indian time: after the prayer meeting, after the feast, when John was ready. It was the middle of June. Twilight and the opening prayers would not come for at least nine hours. I stood on Henry's front porch and looked at the Volvo.

It had been our ship through the nights and days of all our Lame Deer passages and then some. I'd bought it from Tom, hoping to hang on to the good old days. I looked at Henry's car, still parked where I'd left it that night after it carried us down from the Ashland Divide in a hail of marital strife, sparks, and backfires. Beyond it the view contained a few houses across the road and, beyond them, a hill typical of the region: a couple of hundred feet high and one of a progression rising toward the Ashland Divide.

I wondered how many times I'd looked at that hill, how many times I had watched its iron-rich earth turn a vibrant red and gold in the afternoon sun, or watched it glow under stars or moon as the earth does nowhere else. Under stars or moon or cloud, it was that hill I contemplated on long nights in Lame Deer when I couldn't sleep. And on those nights I invariably felt as though I were the only living creature at the center of a landscape without end.

It was a small leap of the imagination from that feeling to the scenario of the high plains 250 years ago. Despite Manifest Destiny, industrialization, and the rest of it, most of that primeval vastness remains. The earth I saw bathed in starlight was the same earth once known only to the Cheyennes and the other Plains tribes. Before the Europeans came, they felt that vastness too and embraced it as their own. And despite the changes brought by the intruders, the Cheyennes still see what they have always seen: the view from Henry's front porch.

I was suddenly aware of my loneliness or, rather, that I was suddenly a stranger in Lame Deer once again. I didn't look at Henry's house or the hill as I drove away. I took it slow all the way into town. I wondered if Dick Littlebear might be there.

I sat on the front porch of the Lame Deer Cafe with half a dozen older Cheyenne men. We shared my cigarettes as we stared at a spot of nothingness located above the rooftop of the IGA across the street. I asked if they'd seen Dick Littlebear. There was silence and then, "I think he lives in Busby." I let it drop. I'd stopped at Dick's trailer on my way down, but it was obvious he hadn't been there for a while. After a longer silence, one man asked, "Do you know Tom West? He has a car just like yours." I admitted knowing Tom without explaining the car and gave each of them a cigarette as I left. Most of them said, "I don't smoke" but put the cigarettes in their shirt pockets anyway.

By two-thirty in the afternoon I was easing the Volvo up the crest of the Ashland Divide, looking for the turnout to Crazy Head Springs. It is one of two public campgrounds between Crow Agency and Belle Fourche, the second at Red Shale in the Custer National Forest. Cheyenne families didn't camp much at Crazy Head, but young people came up on weekends to drink beer and make out. I'd not been there before.

The springs bubble up near the top of the ridge and then push their fingers down, beneath the surface, where they eventually touch and cup themselves into a series of pools, each on a small plateau, all laced together by a maze of trails. From the highway the gravel access road dissolves after about an eighth of a mile. From there the trees crowd in close to the mossy banks of the pools and provide a world of shade—silent but for the distant sound of water.

I drove beyond the end of the road to the first pool, parked on a level spot, got out, and lay down on the moss near the water. It felt cool and good against my back. From somewhere up the ridge I thought I heard voices. Then it was silent, then the voices again—closer that time; they sounded like children. Silence, then voices—farther away—then silence. Nothing—and then the memories and the little ironies that came with them, particularly the ones contained in the box of photographs I'd placed on the ground beside me.

These were my prints from the last 147 negatives in the Marquis collection. Marquis began making photographs in 1922, when he arrived on the reservation as Agency physician, and continued until his death in 1935. His tenure as physician was brief, the problems of treating fourteen hundred Indians scattered over an area of six hundred square miles too frustrating. After ten weeks on the reservation, he resigned his position.

Within a few years he abandoned medicine altogether so that he could devote all his time to writing about the Cheyennes. From 1924 until his death he produced more than a dozen articles and books on the Cheyenne people. These, together with his nearly five hundred photographs, provide an intimate ethnography of the time.

His clear sympathy and respect for the Cheyennes made it possible for him to gather narratives from those who had survived the Cheyenne nadir after the Custer battle and the beginnings of the reservation period. Through their narratives he was able to record important elements of a time now lost to everyone and to revise the accepted accounts of the Custer fight. Moreover, he did it all at a time when there was little or no interest in the Cheyenne people. Indeed, a decade after his death, virtually all his work was out of print, and major efforts still unpublished. After 1955, however, there was renewed interest in his work. By 1976 the efforts of his daughters, several scholars, and Tom Weist had brought all his writings to publication, where they received the recognition they deserved.

As I lay on the moss that afternoon, I wondered if Dr. Marquis ever spent an hour or two at the springs to cool down a bit as he made his rounds during his summer as Agency physician. And I wondered if he too would see the irony in our meeting, decades apart, through the medium we both appreciated as the most precise form of historical record. For it is through photographs that the actuality of those who shaped the history of the West is confirmed and their dimension magnified. We are conceptually richer for the portraits of Sitting Bull, Geronimo, Little Wolf, and the rest because we can see the depth of humanity in those faces and then contemplate the actions of our ancestors with some acuity.

That Marquis and I had been about the same business on the reservation was at least curious, if not ironic. Certainly he had been more organized and purposeful in the endeavor. But as I opened the box and thumbed through the prints again, it was clear that he and I did share love and deep respect for the Cheyenne people.

Marquis also admired the frontier photography of Casey Barthelmess ("Photographer on an Army Mule") and L. A. Huffman. Introduced to Huffman by the city editor of the Billings Gazette, W. H. Banfill, in January 1930, he later visited Huffman in Miles City and talked at length with him. Although he appreciated the artistry of Huffman's work, he recognized that art was not his own calling and did little to hone his photographic skills—though I did find some negatives that he'd attempted to retouch.

But with all deference to "art," what Marquis brought to this work was the gift of the neophyte. Untrained in either ethnography or photography, he was therefore uniquely able to achieve the kind of insight available only to one unfettered by dogma. His writing is as stiff as his camera work, yet he managed to gather data that had escaped others. And with his camera he achieved an intimacy usually reserved for family members who catch each other when they are truly themselves.

More often than not, the shutter clicked when the subject had relinquished the pose, a moment only a friend could recognize. And it was this complete lack of formality that came though his photographs, as if his subjects were merely pausing briefly in their routine to humor the good doctor by holding still so he wouldn't have a blurred image waiting for him at the drugstore.

I looked at the photograph of Iron Teeth. It was one I'd printed several times, hoping to render more than was available from a very underexposed negative. Yet nowhere in the collection is informality, as a prelude to intimacy, more evident than in the picture of Iron Teeth.

She was ninety-two years old in 1926 when he took this picture, and as the oldest woman in the Cheyenne tribe she had survived much, including the deaths of her husband and son, who were killed by white soldiers. She had known the Cheyenne way of life before the final white invasion, and she had lived through their darkest hours, including the Fort Robinson escape and the march north from Oklahoma.

It was then, as they fled across the Nebraska midwinter snow, that her son was killed. Separated from her, he and his little sister hid from the soldiers in a deep crevasse at the edge of a coulee. They stayed there all night, but in the morning the soldiers came back to search the coulee. The boy covered his sister with dirt and leaves and then crawled out; he charged the soldiers, attacked them unarmed, and was killed. The soldiers left without detecting his sister, but the next day, when she crawled out and tried to slip away, she was captured.

Iron Teeth sat before the camera as she wanted to be remembered. With her robe draped around her shoulders, she held the elkhorn hide scraper her husband had given her as a wedding present. It was her most precious possession, and she had carried it with her for seventy-two years. He had never taken another wife and had been faithful to her throughout their marriage. She had notched the scraper to keep track of the ages of their five children. In the picture, her head is bowed over it. Her face, etched with a thousand rivulets of history, is calm.

The photograph and her story are pristine ethnography. But in equal measure they are a statement about the relationship between Marquis and the Cheyennes he respected so well—a relationship she confirmed in the last lines of her story, speaking directly to him:

> I used to cry every time anything reminded me of the killing of my husband and son. But I now have become old enough to talk quietly of them. I used to hate all white people, especially their soldiers. But my heart now has become changed to softer feelings. Some of the white people are good, maybe as good as Indians.

According to our Indian ways, it is considered not right to speak the name of any of our own dead relatives. But mine have been gone many years, and you are well known to us, so I have told you who my husband was. I tell you now the name of my son who was killed: we called him *Mon-see-yo-mon*—Gathering His Medicine. Lots of times, as I sit here alone on the floor with my blanket wrapped about me, I lean forward and close my eyes and think of him standing up out of the pit and fighting the soldiers, knowing that he would be killed, but doing this so that his little sister might get away to safety. Don't you think he was a brave young man?

Marquis's answer, of course, was everywhere in his work. But he did respond directly to Iron Teeth's question and all the questions embedded within it when he spoke of Porcupine, the medicine man who had brought the Ghost Dance to the Cheyennes in the 1890s and was sometimes called the "Messiah Preacher": "Nobility of character is an inherent trait, not a quality conferred by college degree. Long ago—before we had colleges, before we had books, before we had even an alphabet—there were gentlemen among mankind. This Messiah Preacher was of such breed."

I had seen all of them, gentlemen and gentlewomen, represented in 497 photographs, and looking through them again confirmed my first impression: the collection was indeed a family album. Marquis may have seen that too, for he made a wonderful shot of Porcupine and his wife looking at a framed series of his photographs of themselves and their relatives. I recognized the pleasure on their faces; I'd seen it on the faces of John Woodenlegs and the others at the meeting when I brought the first 150 prints for their approval.

I, of course, had first seen the pictures in ignorance, and so as each emerged in the developer the significant and the ordinary were equally anonymous. At the meeting, however, anonymity was quickly replaced by instantaneous recognition. John saw himself in one photo as an adolescent member of the Lame Deer baseball team. And, in addition to very famous men who had fought Custer, there were friends and neighbors side by side within the circle of community that had held them all together.

Beyond their delight, however, was the uncanny accuracy with
which they were able to identify people in those photos, many of
which seemed mere blobs of underexposed silver. As they did so,
of course, anecdotes about this one or that could not be suppressed,
and I was astonished to realize that the elders I had recently photographed were young people in the Marquis collection. He and I had
registered the polarities of a generation.

As the last of that first set were viewed, we explored ways to display the photographs for the tribe. After many suggestions were
made as to the best place, I offered the proposal that they be displayed in glass cases to protect them from touching and possible
theft. And with that a sudden pall covered the room. At last, John
Woodenlegs looked sternly at me and said: "Cheyennes don't steal!!
We just borrow it for one year!!"

There was a long silence while I wobbled in uncertainty and
then a general whoop and laughter. And their laughter echoed
in my mind's ear as I remembered challenging John's ability to recognize and identify featureless forms in many of the prints. I'd
even gone so far as to ask others outside the committee, including
Irene, to identify those blobs. Incredibly, they consistently agreed.
When I asked John if he would be able to identify anyone he'd
known, Indian or white, in a photograph as poor as some of these,
he thought for a long minute and said, "I don't know—you white
people all look the same to me."

And then the laughter was echoing outside my memory, off the
surface of the many pools at Crazy Head Springs. It carried the hollow sound of memory with it but was louder this time. I stood and
moved up the path a little, looking and listening—silence. I returned to my mossy bank and the box of photographs and thought
about how Marquis and Porcupine became partners in his fieldwork, not unlike Henry and me.

There was a photograph of Porcupine in the box, the first Marquis ever took of him. He is posed with three others in front of the
old Agency hotel in Lame Deer. The four were all respected elders
and chiefs: Laban Little Wolf, Hairy Hand, Big Beaver, and Porcupine. Laban Little Wolf was nephew to the elder Little Wolf, who,
along with Morning Star, led the march north from Oklahoma and
had fought in the Custer battle. Big Beaver and Hairy Hand were
also famous warriors, and of course it was Porcupine who journeyed
to Pyramid Lake, Nevada, in 1889 to meet Wovoka, the messiah, and

brought the Ghost Dance to the Northern Cheyennes. Until his death in 1929 at age eighty-one he was the most revered of Cheyenne medicine men and teachers.

The photograph was taken in 1922 during Marquis's first summer on the reservation. Marquis saw the four elders seated at a table reserved for Indians in the hotel. He asked his interpreter, a Cheyenne named Black Stone, to tell Porcupine he wanted to take his picture. After some discussion, Porcupine demanded cash payment for the sitting. Marquis pleaded immunity because he was Agency physician and prohibited from such transactions. Porcupine pleaded poverty. Marquis offered the money as a gift. They agreed on the sum of twenty-five cents. But when Porcupine stepped out of the hotel, the other old men followed and lined up with him for the picture. No mention was made about paying them. When the photograph was made, Marquis gave Porcupine a silver dollar and had Black Stone explain his intention.

Porcupine reflected for a moment and then went back into the Hotel. He came out with four silver quarters and gave one to each of the other men. He held up the fourth quarter, close to his face, studied it carefully and then stepped to the side. He handed it to White Hawk, then eighty years old, who was sitting on the ground in the shade of the hotel. Black Stone translated for Porcupine: "My friend White Hawk is older—and poorer than I am."

I looked up from the photograph into the pale shafts of sunlight that sliced the shade and cut bright windows into the water. I listened for the laughter—nothing, only the sound of my own breathing. I replaced the picture in the file and searched for the one of Black Bird.

In the prairie grass in front of a one-room log cabin he sits in profile to the camera, one leg stretched out in front, out of the frame, the other tucked under him. His clothing is plain, the denim trousers and khaki work shirt typical of 1928 working men, somewhat threadbare at the edges. He is wearing a light-colored scarf on his head, knotted at the forehead. Behind his ear a small braid of his hair just touches his shoulder. His lean, muscular frame belies his sixty-two years. He is poised, alert to a presence outside the normal range of awareness. His eyes are fixed on some space beyond the frame. His awareness of the photographer is somewhat ambiguous. He sustains a certain diffidence while his outstretched hands and long, graceful fingers hold a little girl at her midriff—a toddler, perhaps his granddaughter. Her pudgy fingers are laced together, both thumbs in her mouth. Her eyes are directed down at her hands, and her body, even within the circle of his hands, appears uncertain about its new-found balance. A slight breeze ruffles the hair at the crown of her head; the shutter's release has transformed it into downy fluff.

I looked at the photograph and realized that no one could tell (except a Cheyenne who understood what his head scarf represented) that this was a holy man, the Keeper of the Sacred Tipi and the Sacred Buffalo Hat. Nor could anyone see, even those who knew him then, his despair over the inability of his community to support him and the disgrace he had to endure from defiling his position by supporting himself with labor. The material poverty of the tribe was his spiritual horror. His predecessor, Rock Roads, had also endured this humiliation. Marquis photographed him as well and often heard him apologize with great sadness, "Christ— no flour, no bread, nothing. Christ—my wife no got anything eat. Christ—new tipi forty dollars. Christ—what a man do?"

A crow snarled at me from the treetops; the voices followed quickly on it, and I jumped. The voices called and the crow cried again as it took flight and laughter faded under wing sound. I heard my heart beating. There were children up there at the top of the ridge, I was sure.

I listened again and then put the picture of Black Bird back in the file. Just behind it was a photograph of the Busby Boarding School, a group of girls on the playground in front of the classroom building and dormitory. There is something odd, unsettling, about it. The photographer has obviously interrupted, invaded the scene, and his subjects are uncertain, uneasy, the way we are after being told to relax and act "natural."

In the foreground, four girls hold onto ladder swings attached to a center pole and carousel to make a flying merry-go-round. They hold on with one hand and lean as if ready to mount and take flight—but they look too posed. Three of them face the camera, two at the extremities of the frame and one in the center who willfully engages the photographer with a posed smile. The one on the right leans against the swing chain, her face turned downward, her expression sullen. The girl on the left mirrors the pose but looks straight into the camera or, perhaps, through and beyond it. At the center of the frame, with her back to the camera, the fourth hangs

from the ladder with her body cantilevered over the mud puddle that
circles the base of the swing set. Behind them, eight girls stand in
a row facing the camera, each caught between turning away and
the curiosity that compels them to stare at the photographer.

The light is the light that comes after rain, the sky like gray chalk,
and in that light the girls' collective isolation seems pronounced.
They all wear the same faded plain white shifts, dingy from numer-
ous washings. Their hair is uniformly styled: bobbed at the ears,
straight bangs across the forehead. The dresses don't quite fit, obviously recycled from lots with age-graded sizing, purchased in ad-
vance; one or two display a simple print or stripe. Beneath, each
wears black knee socks and high button shoes that all seem too
large.

The photograph attempts to show schoolgirls at play but reveals instead a collective hesitation at the edge of play, at the edge
of the photographic pose—at the edge of identity.

The school in the photograph was a model of the Indian boarding school whose progenitor was the Hampton Institute in Virginia,
founded by Samuel Armstrong, a former missionary and comman-
der of a Negro regiment in the Civil War. Hampton, among the first
boarding schools for freed slaves, became in 1878 the first off-
reservation school for Native Americans. Its first students had all
been hostages at Fort Marion in St. Augustine, Florida, during the
final Indian wars on the southern plains: one was Arapaho, five
Kiowa, and eleven Cheyenne. Once at Hampton, they were segre-
gated by sex, and the men were placed under the care of one of
Hampton's recent graduates, their new "housefather," Booker T.
Washington.

I looked at the photograph of the Busby Boarding School girls
and wondered how those girls had fared under the regimen of cultural indoctrination. And I wondered what the future author of
Up from Slavery thought, as housefather, when he did bed-check on
his Native American charges each night at Hampton. I wondered if
the girls in the back row were breaking the rules and talking with
each other, in whispers, in Cheyenne. I was sure I could hear them
giggling and talking. I was sure it was getting louder.

"Hey Mister! Give us a ride to Ashland!"

I caught the photograph just before it fell into the water and
stared at them. A boy, about five, a girl, maybe eight, stared back
across the pool at me. They were holding hands, their sides pressed

together, utterly still, black eyes fixed on mine, fiercely sustaining the demand over my silence. He wore threadbare jeans and T-shirt; she, a faded print dress. Both were barefoot and a little crusty from a day's worth of mud adventures, their very black hair still damp and shining with spring water.

We stared at each other for a long time. At last I asked where their parents were. They said nothing, but their eyes remained fixed and bored into me. I encouraged them to wait. Surely their parents would come for them soon, I insisted. "No, no, they left us here this morning—they won't come back."

I held my ground but felt ambivalent and very uneasy. Children often experience time distortion, and I was unwilling to believe they'd been abandoned. I offered a compromise: "Stay here awhile and wait—I'm sure they'll come. If they don't show up, I'll give you a ride."

The boy was tired and started to sit down, but his sister pulled him up by his arm. He whined a little and she scolded him in Cheyenne. I lay back in the moss with my hands behind my head and hoped they'd relax too. "C'mon Mister, give us a ride." Her tone was less demanding, a plea for sympathy. I didn't answer.

They stood and stared at me for another long time and then sat down. I assured them once more and closed my eyes. And then I heard their feet slip into the water, and the boy laughed a little. They spoke softly to each other for a minute and then it was very quiet.

Quiet—then suddenly, as if touched by some fairytale magician, I fell through the moss into a void and slept the sleep of stones. And just as suddenly I awoke in a surge of parental anxiety and panic.

They were gone. I wanted to call to them but realized I hadn't asked their names. I scanned the area and listened—nothing, not even the sound of water. As I ventured up each of the paths a short distance and paused and listened and called out and heard my "Hello" fall into nothingness, I wondered if I'd dreamed them. My memory was already distorting them, casting them into a tale of lost children from another time, never found, whose ghosts now haunt the paths and pools of Crazy Head Springs. I bathed my face in spring water and was suddenly horrified by the prospect that they had indeed been abandoned and were out there on the high-way, hitchhiking.

I drove slowly down the long straight grade and stopped at ter-
rifying places where the road skirted the precipice with only inches
of shoulder and looked down into the tangle of brush and pine for
that which I could not bear to visualize, briefly gratified when they
weren't there, then tormented by thoughts of abduction. When I
finally crossed the Tongue River into Ashland, I was in despair. I
stopped in front of a cafe. I'd inquire within; perhaps they'd passed
by, perhaps they were known.

And then I saw them a hundred yards down the road, walking
hand in hand, their bare feet making little dust storms around their
legs, their bodies shimmering within the heat waves. I watched
them pause in front of the other bar in town, then enter, stay inside
briefly, then come out and continue down the road. As I turned toward the cafe, I was sure I saw the girl look back at me, and I was
sure those black eyes found me through the heat and dust.

Inside the cafe I drank ice water and measured the pros and
cons of eating peyote on an empty stomach or eating the Blue Plate
Special first. I chose the latter. The cook and I were alone. It was six
o'clock—three hours until the prayer meeting. I left anyway and
headed back up the divide.

As I passed the Ashland Bar, the clientele were making the afternoon changeover per schedule. Half a dozen cowboys adjusted
their white straw hats and sunglasses before climbing into their
pickups. I looked in the rearview mirror as I crossed the bridge.
The children were gone.

Two-thirds of the way up the divide the dirt road to the meeting
place veered off to the right, followed the crest, and then leveled off
onto a small plateau. A few cars were there, John's and that of the
woman who was putting up the meeting to bless her new home.
The new house was down in a grove of cottonwoods below the
plateau, so the tipi dominated the landscape with its new canvas
shining in the low angle of the sun. I got out of the car, leaned
against a headlight, and waited.

It was June 1976. In a few days the state would mark the one
hundredth anniversary of the Custer fight and, a few after that, the
bicentennial of the nation. For many springtimes before either of
those events, the Cheyennes came to this place, roughly between
the prayer meeting tipi and the Big Horn River, to hunt the buffalo.
They returned year after year because the hunting was good, and

they knew, therefore, that Sweet Medicine had been right and that if they heeded his words they would prosper forever. And so, even after their world fell apart, they returned to this land because they knew and still know that life and health are possible only here.

On certain evenings, when the cross-light finds a certain angle, it's easy to see why. On those evenings the twilight rises slowly up the long spears of prairie grass, its progress measured in shades of umber and gold until it hesitates at the tips, where, for an instant, stars appear. Then the ground goes blue, and cool moisture rises to fill the air with the smell of grass and earth. And then the sun takes the last few degrees of its arc and draws a thin white line at the place where the finite and the infinite meet. They touch briefly and then there is stillness, a stillness drifting in and out of the cries of nighthawks and the shudder of bat wings.

The sun was gone and the stillness descended. I hadn't noticed the arrival of cars or the passage of people around me as they moved toward the tipi until I took a long deep breath of cool air, moist with prairie grass, and was awakened to the sound.

The call of the eagle-bone whistle insinuated itself into the cries of the nighthawks while the people lined up behind John, who began his prayers of invocation at the first of the four cardinal directions. The tipi, now singed with twilight, began to glow from within. Still standing at a distance, I watched and was convinced for an instant that we were the only people on earth and that we could, through the course of this night, remember what it was like when human beings and the natural order were in accord. I walked through the dark grass and took my place in line.

Inside, John greeted me, and I found my place next to Francis Black Horse. He had been the drummer at all the meetings I'd attended and his fine drumming had no doubt been requested by the sponsor of this one. Directly across from me a young Cheyenne man, perhaps twenty years old, eyed me carefully through wire-rimmed hippie-style glasses. He wore a western shirt and leather vest with feathers hanging from the conchos. His long dark hair was impeccably braided, the ends tied with red yarn. He was lean and self-assured and greeted me curtly just as the opening prayers began. I nodded curtly in response and then took the sack of tobacco and papers and made my cigarette for the offering. I smoked and felt the strain of the day yield to the familiar habits of ritual. I'd been to several meetings, but this time I truly felt at ease. When I placed my tobacco offering on the altar next to John's, I looked at the young man again. This time he smiled.

And then the music and the aromatic mixture of cedar and cottonwood and the sacred plant enveloped me and gave me the night to relive the day when Tom and Henry and I took the Kirby-Decker road to Sheridan. The peyote songs rose and fell all around my memory of that day until the medicine brought it to me with all the clarity of what had been.

It was one of those days that come suddenly on the heels of August's "dog days" to banish them and declare the inevitability of autumn. These are the days when light and atmosphere converge to part the veil covering the tender underbelly of the landscape, when frost lurks in the shadows of dawn like a voyeur and then slinks out into the sunlight to mix warmth and chill into an elixir that stains the leaves and your cheeks with seduction.

It was that kind of day, and it kept our voices low, murmuring, like conversation heard in the next room. As we drove south out of Birney Village, the landscape and its peculiar enchantments seemed to reinforce all that was unspoken among us.

It was the first time that Tom and I had journeyed to Lame Deer and found Henry at home alone. He was laconic and at loose ends, the way married men are when their wives go away, uncertain about how to move or behave in the absence of that primary reference and more than a little astonished at how deeply habituated they are to the love of the woman.

But Henry's passion for Irene was laced with melancholy. As arthritis progressively ravaged her joints and her days became litanies of pain, intimacy was often impossible. And so she couldn't help falling into the fear that her man, clearly the most virile of men, had found comfort elsewhere. Eventually, his need and her anguish would collide, and she would accuse him and they would fight.

They'd fought over it a few days before Tom and I arrived; Irene had gone to Forsyth in a huff. He was doubly despondent because the object of his suspected liaison was one whose reputation for universal accommodation had attained symbolic status on the reservation; her name, in fact, was the preferred nominalization for sexual deviancy wherever it occurred. But for Henry, who admitted the occasional fit of desperation, the proposal was ludicrous.

Irene knew this, so within the push and shove of their private wars, reference to the queen of whores was an ultimate weapon, one that would end the fight and force one or both of them to quit the field.

For Tom and me it was the easy way to skirt the issue and avoid talking about the things men would rather not talk about. It was easier to lighten his mood by taking cheap shots at the whore and affirming that we would never bend so low—not in deference to our marriage vows but because the experience itself would be so re-volting. And then, to celebrate our sexist brotherhood, we decided to drive to Sheridan to stalk the elusive half-rack of Budweiser and all the fixin's for a feast. By the time we got to Birney Village, Henry was laughing easily, and we had declared women unnecessary—at least for the weekend.

We paused along the Tongue River, below the dam, and skipped rocks across it from a gravel bar and wandered the shoreline in search of caddis tubes and symbolic driftwood. Henry hushed us so we could watch a sage hen and her chicks march nervously to the river for a drink. And while we watched, he nostalgically wished for his .22, reminding us that his marksmanship included the abil-ity to shoot the heads off wild turkeys and grouse at fifty yards. Al-ready apprised of his night hunting skills, we turned and blessed the grouse after reminding them of their good fortune in the pres-ence of an unarmed yet great hunter. We decided to buy pork chops for dinner when we got to Sheridan.

On the road again we inhaled the new crisp air through open win-dows and found the words we thought we didn't know and spoke generously of Irene with Henry. She'd come back and all would be forgiven. And he would continue to help her as he always had.

We knew Henry loved Irene simply because she was Irene, but we couldn't really say that, any more than we could say that we loved each other. And so we let our affection spread itself beneath our words and between our silences. Having felt them was enough. We turned our affection out—into the dream around us.

It was a dream that had begun twelve thousand years before us. For then, as the ice that had carved the basin we traveled through receded and left the massive lake behind it, the first colonists began to arrive. They were Henry's ancestors, the Paleo-Indians, and surely, as they stepped off the glacier onto the savanna, they must have caught their breath. Stretching out before them was a diversity of flora and fauna whose opulence has not been witnessed since.

As representatives of a fledgling humanity whose total world population was roughly eight million strong, these colonists were the vanguard of the restless human spirit, mindlessly motivated except for the need to search beyond the next hill for better times. Yet one wonders what stories and flights of imagination supported a migration so massive in scope, so daunting.

Like the European colonists who came nine thousand years later, the Paleo-Indians saw a world that went on forever. The sheer vastness of the basin and the overwhelming numbers of beasts, all ignorant of the human predator, could hardly have inspired conservation or wildlife management. Transfixed, as they must have been, within the illusion of the infinite and its immediate rewards, projection beyond the next meal, the next feast, or the next hunt would have been impossible.

Tom and Henry and I could still see much of what those Paleo-Indians saw. The basin itself, even with the population explosion of recent history, was much the same. The great inland sea, of course, was gone, but most of the small birds and hawks and vultures and eagles remained, as did the butterflies and other insects, coniferous and deciduous trees, small mammals, elk and antelope. But of all those things, it was the expanse of the great American basin before us that finally compelled us to stop and walk its surface to the base of a massive sand-rock island.

Beneath our feet were the remainders of what those ancient colonists saw. Deep within the compressed sediment and layers of erosion were the bones of humanity that reached back to the end of the Pleistocene era, commingled with bits of charcoal from cooking fires and the bones of Colombian imperial and woolly mammoths, enormous flightless birds, and ground sloths.

Henry didn't like to talk about bones, but he knew they were there. He said his grandparents had told stories about the time when their ancestors wore great hairy robes to keep out the cold. We wondered if there still might be stories, as yet ungathered, among the remaining indigenous tribes, about the last of the mammoths and the people's response to their passing. And then, as surely as we knew their traces existed below us, we were sure we felt them respond to our wondering as we circumnavigated the base of the butte.

Its facade rose more than one hundred feet above us, but behind it the island had collapsed into a rubble of enormous sandstone slabs and pillars. We felt the hollow vibration from subterranean caves as we stepped through the ruins. Erosion had carved a catacomb beneath the surface, shielded in some places by only a few inches of brittle earth. And as we walked, the void beneath seemed to answer our footsteps, as if we had awakened the heartbeats of chthonic spirits from the unopened vaults of time and they were following us.

I was sure I felt their rhythm through the soles of my feet. I looked at Henry. He knew them. His body took on an alertness and poise I'd never seen. I felt the hair rise on the back of my neck as an enormous magpie circled and jeered and came to rest on a large sandstone obelisk. It fluttered and blinked and stared us down. And then Henry's arms went out like wings and he made them dip high and low while his body and feet danced and the earth drum sounded louder and louder until four dust devils spun around us, blinding us.

And then silence and stillness amid the clear, crisp, autumnal air.

The magpie was gone. Henry looked at me curiously and said, "It's hollow under here, we should get off." I was speechless, wobbling between mirage and reality. I wanted to comment about the magpie and the earth drum, but then Tom took a step forward and we all froze as the earth issued a long bass tone followed by the singular sound of one stone dropping into a deep pool. Henry muttered something in Cheyenne, and Tom and I said "Right!" as if we understood him. We all moved carefully down to the car.

We drove on and took turns looking in the rearview mirror. The island seemed to follow us all the way to Sheridan, and its memory kept us silent through the purchase of our feast and a week's worth of groceries for Henry. We added a second half-rack to the larder on our way out of town and remained silent until the road dropped down along the foothills of the Wolf Mountains into the valley of Rosebud Creek.

We stopped where the road crosses the creek to stretch and quench our thirst. Near the bridge is a small church tucked amid the cottonwoods and willows. A few miles farther up the road is the site of the Battle of the Rosebud. Tom and I surveyed the church and talked about the battle while Henry wandered down to the creek.

The Cheyennes call that battle "Where the Girl Saved Her Brother." It happened nine days before the Custer fight and had he heard about it, he might well have considered alternative strategies.

As it was, on June 16, 1876, Gen. George Crook led thirteen hundred soldiers into the valley of the Rosebud, where an equal number of Sioux and Cheyenne warriors attacked them. Crazy Horse had tried one of his decoy maneuvers; it failed to fool General Crook, but he did split his troops into two groups. The fighting went on all day, and even though Crook weathered the attack and had a slight advantage, he had his men dig in, take a defensive position, and wait for the Indians to quit the field.

At the height of the battle the celebrated Cheyenne warrior Comes in Sight lost his horse to a soldier's bullet. On foot, he was quickly cornered by several of Crook's scouts. Seeing the danger, his sister, Buffalo Calf Woman, rode straight through the center of the fighting to her brother's side; Comes in Sight jumped on behind her, and they managed to escape.

Finally, when they saw that the soldiers weren't going to attack anymore, the Indians withdrew. The next day, Crook's forces left for Goose Creek near present-day Sheridan, Wyoming, where the general and his men rested and went fishing. Somehow Crook didn't bother to send a warning to Custer about the size or capability of the Indian forces gathered at the Little Big Horn.

Tom and I talked about them as we walked up the road in search of Henry. I paused and made a photograph of the Rosebud snaking its way through the willows just as the sun dropped lower and turned the water into quicksilver. And then, as if in memory of the battle and therefore right on cue, we heard a "whoop" from the creek bottom.

Henry stood waist deep in the Rosebud, dripping wet in the wake of the splash, the water in front of him still churning. "There's a beaver! I almost caught him!" Sweeping his drenched hair from his forehead, he squatted down and slapped the surface of the pool with his palm. In seconds the water churned, and the enormous tail smacked it hard and doused him again as the beaver rolled and disappeared. He stood up and laughed and whooped and laughed again while the setting sun turned him gold and glistening. And then it dropped quickly behind the hill, and he stood there for a long moment in the half-light of the valley, and I saw him as I never would again. He was, to the depths of his cells, at home—and he was beautiful.

We rode the echo of his final whoop and laughter up onto the plateau and headed back toward Birney. I looked out into the Tongue River basin and at the mountains beyond and saw the sun inching toward them and made Tom stop the car. I ran like a madman to the crest of a hill to catch the sunlight as it winked over the edge of the mountains and traced the broad sweep and bend of the river. In seconds it was gone, but I had caught it. And then it was my turn to stand there inside the wonder of my own existence.

I looked back at the car just as the sunset illuminated its interior and revealed Tom and Henry as silhouettes above the valley. Within that instant before darkness at last claims the sky we were encased in a bulb of twilight, a muted nimbus suspended above a world wherein the breath of men is sweetened by the taste of children's laughter.

The tipi door swung open, and the morning light carried the beaver dam and Tom and Henry out into the sun. An elbow on my right nudged my ribs to awaken me to the passage of meat, fruit, and corn. I handed the cups to my left, still caught in the uncertainty of after-dream. I was not sure whether I had slept or not, or if I had behaved appropriately through a night I could not remember. But then I looked to my right and saw Hestahae, and the memory rushed back.

Through much of the night he had sat smiling the way he always did as the drum and staff passed him again and again. Each time I watched, and each time it was more and more obvious that he wanted to sing. And then, somewhere amid the swirl of drumbeats and prayers long after midnight, Francis Black Horse moved and took a seat next to Hestahae. There was a long, uncomfortable silence after Hestahae seized the drum and handed it to Francis and held the staff. Some people laughed a bit and covered their mouths with their hands. The young man with hippie glasses looked at John and said, "He wants to sing."

John smiled as he and Hestahae exchanged signs over the sounds from Hestahae's cleft palate, which emphasized the language of his hands. At last Francis rose to his knees and began to drum. Incredibly, Hestahae, who was deaf and mute, sang—and the song soared. He sang, and it was the voice of God.

I looked at him in the morning light with renewed amazement. Then I looked down at my cup of corn and knew that the medicine was still with me: I saw through all the kernels, straight down to those few resting at the bottom of the cup. And then a wave of laughter began to rise up from my belly, the kind of laughter that must, if expressed at all, break out into weeping. At that edge, I coughed and choked it down and looked across the circle at the young man in braids. He shook his head slowly and said, "I guess we're gonna have to teach these white people how to eat peyote." There was general laughter as we all ate our corn.

And then it was time again for each person to offer a prayer of thanks or a story from the passage of the night we had all shared. At last, John looked at me and introduced me to the group. He talked about my friendship with Tom and my work on the Marquis photographs. When he finished, he looked at me the way he always did when he expected a speech.

I began by thanking him again for inviting me, not only to this meeting but to all the ones I had attended. I reminded him about my first meeting and how honored I'd been by that invitation, which came so soon after I had started visiting the reservation. And then I shared with the group the experiences I'd had at that meeting. I told them how the medicine had helped me remember my childhood experiences with the Métis children in Great Falls. I told them as best I could how those early experiences had haunted me all my life and that perhaps the peyote medicine and the prayer meeting had brought them to me again for a reason. I told them that each of the meetings I'd attended had taught me a great deal, and maybe those children I'd met so long ago were, in part, responsible for my coming to Lame Deer. I wanted them to know that I hoped the small contribution I'd made would be helpful, and I asked them to remember Henry Tall Bull in their prayers.

When I finished, John smiled and said, "That's good." And then he began his morning prayers.

Later, the young man and I stood together as John blessed the food before the feast. We talked a bit while we waited for the elders to be served, and I told him more about the Marquis project. He said, "We love this country here, this land. Most people think it's empty and ugly. But they don't know how to see it. Cheyennes think it's beautiful—that's why we stay here."

I lounged in the grass with the others and enjoyed the feast, and then John and I walked out away from the tipi to my car. As I handed him the box of prints, my throat closed down, and I felt the tears rise. I had let go of too many things and said goodbye too many ways over the previous thirty-six hours. I knew I could not manage saying goodbye to him.

Here was the man whose complete religious faith had permeated all my journeys to Lame Deer. He, perhaps more than any man of his generation, had doggedly fought major battles with white bureaucracy to rejuvenate his people, and he had won most of them. In keeping with his status as medicine man and chief, he had trusted me, a white man, with an invaluable portion of his people's heritage and endured their praise and criticism for it with good cheer.

He looked through the prints and smiled. "Your work is good. You have helped us a lot. But the Cheyenne people are still a poor people, and the things we need are expensive."

It was not going to be easy. I looked at the ground and said, "I know, John—I know and I . . . " But I couldn't finish the sentence. I had started to say "and I will come back," but I couldn't get it out; I knew I wasn't coming back, but I couldn't say that either. I think he knew it, though.

"Us Cheyennes are tough people," he said, "and peyote is good medicine." On that we shook hands, and I turned away and drove out and over the Ashland Divide for the last time.

8

It was Sunday morning. I eased the Volvo down from the divide and glided into Lame Deer where I was embraced by a universal Sunday morning stillness sustained and punctuated by bells. People were starting to arrive at the Mennonite church on the hill, and I saw Joe Walks Along circumnavigating the building as I drove by. I coasted to a stop in front of the cafe. It was closed. I'd hoped to get a coffee for the road.

I got out and leaned on the side of the car. The IGA was closed too, but there was some movement next door, inside the gas station. Two days before it had been difficult to come here at all, and now I found it nearly impossible to leave. I looked toward the place where the old Agency had stood and at the hill behind it. It was called Squaw Hill, and it is the place where the last of the suicide warriors met their fate. Their story was Henry's favorite. I looked at the hill and wondered if he wanted their story to be his.

By September 1890 the Tongue River Reserve was nearly six years old. During those first difficult seasons all the Northern Cheyennes' attempts at dry-land farming had failed. Without crops or means to hunt, they were entirely dependent on government rations for subsistence. Those rations were often short, and the people were starving.

All around them the white ranchers encroached, in protest against the establishment of the reservation; they grazed their cattle and established illegal homesteads near disputed boundaries. The men of the tribe were desperate and humiliated. Their traditional role as providers for their families had been nullified; their ceremonies celebrating manhood were outlawed. There was no game. There was no Sun Dance.

Early in September 1890, Head Chief, then twenty-five years old, and his friend John Young Mule, a thirteen-year-old orphan, went hunting. And, not unlike a Cheyenne couple who went night hunting some eighty years later, they found themselves along the banks of Lame Deer Creek in the morning, empty-handed and staring at the plump cattle belonging to a homesteader named Gaffney. They killed one of Gaffney's cows and butchered it on the spot.

They were barely on the trail back to camp when they encountered Gaffney's nephew, Hugh Boyle. He saw the fresh meat on their packhorse and accused them. Head Chief promptly shot him dead. They hauled his body into the hills, hid it, and camped for the night. The next morning they made their way to the camp of the great chief American Horse.

Unknown to Head Chief and Young Mule, the scene of the murder had been discovered by the Indian police, and the search had already reached American Horse's camp. The camp was a shambles when they got there. The search party had torn it apart looking for evidence. The police and white soldiers threatened American Horse with prison if he did not tell all he knew about the killing, and other Cheyenne camps were worried that they too would be attacked.

Head Chief told American Horse what had happened with Hugh Boyle and said that he wanted no harm to come to Cheyenne women and children because of him. He told American Horse what he wanted: "Go down to the Agency. Tell them I killed the boy. Tell them on the next ration day—next Friday—I will be there. Tell them to be ready and I will play with the soldiers at that time. I will come in shooting—let them try to stop me. They will never hang me. I will die like a man." Head Chief went back to his father's camp, gathered his war clothes, and headed off toward Lame Deer. During the next several days he was protected from capture by his friends in the Elk Horn society. On the Thursday night before ration day, he feasted with his friends and vowed he would ride through the soldiers. Shortly before dawn Young Mule approached him and made his own vow: "When you are dead, I will have nothing. I will die too."

On Friday, September 13, at noon, the Cheyenne people assembled at Lame Deer Agency to collect the rations that would not last: beans, coffee, flour, and a few ounces of meat. Suddenly, at the top of the hill behind the Agency, Head Chief appeared, mounted and wearing a great white war bonnet. Young Mule was with him. Together, they charged down the hill, firing into the line of soldiers and police waiting below. Young Mule was shot dead in front of the line, but Head Chief rode through the column and their bullets, untouched, just as he had vowed. Then he turned and faced them again. The soldiers shot him down.

Some say the remains of Head Chief and Young Mule were buried at the top of Squaw Hill by white people from the Agency. I took a long look at it that morning. As suicide warriors, they had chosen death with honor as preferable to a life of dependency and impotence. They saw the assimilated life offered by the white man as a humiliation, an assault on their manhood, and so they preferred integrity to survival.

I first heard Head Chief's story from Henry on that February day when we all drove out of Lame Deer in search of Henry's sandstone woman. I wondered what the people who lined up for rations on that September morning thought as they watched those two young men charge into the line of soldiers. Did they see it as an act of futility and desperation brought on by difficult times? Or did they see it as Head Chief and Young Mule intended: the final acts of bravery by men who were still men?

I was still staring up at the hill when one of the regulars climbed the stairs to the cafe and spoke to me, "He's not open yet. It's Sunday. He goes to church at St. Labre's." I nodded and said "Good morning." The old man took his place in one of the chairs on the porch, and we both looked across the street at the IGA. A few women were there, waiting for it to open.

I too was waiting—for what, I didn't know. Nor did I know what I should do next. I felt desolate and guilty about leaving John and Irene and the others. I was more uncertain than ever about how anyone might do good for another. And as I searched within myself for minute particulars that might still be offered, I found little left for me to give. I lingered in front of the Lame Deer Cafe, finally, because I didn't know how to leave.

I looked the other way, up Highway 212 toward the Ashland Divide. At the end of its long reach was Bear Butte, the Cheyenne sacred mountain. To the southeast was Pine Ridge Agency and the site of the Wounded Knee massacre. Big Foot and his Ghost

Dancers had perished there along the creek bottom three months after Head Chief and Young Mule made their suicide run down Squaw Hill. Both events had marked the end of the struggle for freedom on the plains by the Sioux and Cheyennes.

I turned away from the hill and the road and watched the town come to life. The citizens of Lame Deer were going about their business on a beautiful Sunday morning in June, moving through routines that clearly gave them pleasure, practicing the daily art of simply being Cheyenne. I remembered the words of the young man at the peyote meeting: "The Cheyenne people love this land— that's why we stay here."

And then the old one on the porch of the cafe spoke again.

"You live around here?"

"No, I'm from Missoula. I've just been visiting."

"Mmmm—is that your car?"

"Yeah, it's mine."

"Mmmm—there was a white man used to live here—he had a car like that, Volvo. It's a good one."

"Yeah, it's a good one."

"Mmmm—you're going home now?"

"Yeah, home."

"Mmmm—it's a beautiful day to drive home."

"Yes it is."

Two more older men came to join him on the porch, and they sat and conversed in the way that older Cheyenne men enjoy. And I, lingering within the subdued rhythm of their speech, was overwhelmed by the grief I had suppressed for so long, the grief I had been unable to share with Irene Tall Bull.

And at the terrible center of my grief was the realization that the long sordid history of deceit that has defined Indian-white relationships in Montana, the history I so liberally and frequently condemned, the one in which I placed Henry Tall Bull's death as yet another consequence of its persistence—that history also led directly to me. And with that recognition there came a darker epiphany. For in that moment, as I observed a Lame Deer Sunday morning through my own tears, my complicity in Henry Tall Bull's death seemed all too evident.

It seemed obvious that I had behaved the way the white man always does. In my efforts to prove to Henry that I was not like those I condemned and that I was his ally in the ongoing struggles of his people, I drank with him. In my efforts to refute the stigma of the drunk Indian, I convinced myself that we were engaged in harmless social drinking. When it became evident that his struggle with alcohol was out of control, I turned away.

Although I tried to help him in many ways (my questionable ability to be of actual help notwithstanding), I did not try to help him stop drinking. Instead, I did what I was about to do again. I went home.

And then with a force equal to that epiphany a dust devil spun across the road, hovered at my feet, and stung my tears. I held still and wondered if the old men on the porch saw it or saw me weeping. And then it half collapsed as it spun away and slithered into nothing at the edge of the road. The Cheyennes say you shouldn't walk through dust devils; they are lost spirits.

I wiped my eyes and moved toward the car. The old men on the porch looked at me and nodded as I got in and backed away from the cafe. They knew about dust devils, but they hadn't seen me cry.

As I drove across Lame Deer Creek I was no longer certain that it was indeed my last time, my last day in Lame Deer. But it was certain that I would spend the rest of my life trying to sift the meaning from all my experiences there. And I would also have to confront the inexorable precision of history and Henry Tall Bull's death—indeed, of death itself. The question for me then was (and still is), what, if anything, can be said or done once that precision is acknowledged?

When I drove out of Lame Deer that last day I found the answer to be, just as precisely—nothing. I had nothing to say and did not know what to do. We can circle the graves of those who have died needlessly for as long as we can bear it and then try to find our way to the edges of the inexplicable and the inexorable and hope that from these, other words as precise as death will come—words that will turn us again toward the inexhaustible well of life. We do not fear death as much as we fear knowing that it, and therefore life, is meaningless. Because if it is all meaningless, without purpose or design, then we don't know if we can love life anyway.

On that last day in Lame Deer I didn't know that I would spend the next twenty years circling Henry Tall Bull's grave, nor that I would be ambushed again and again by dust devils when I least expected them: at parties, in an ordinary conversation with a friend, in dreams, within the fading light of certain landscapes. And each time, I was beset by denial, anger, and recrimination until I was left wondering if Henry, even with all the help in the world, would have saved himself—for in the end, he was the only one who could. But that conclusion, like the intolerable fact of his death, offered no solace or understanding.

And so, at the edge of Henry's grave, I must decide what meaning, if there can be any at all, I can take with me now, having arrived at last through this writing at the place where, indeed, white men fear to tread.

I drove out of Lame Deer that last day with the bitter taste of peyote and the intolerable fresh in my mouth. And now, remembering, I can understand how my last day in Lame Deer was the beginning of a journey that would lead me back to where it all began so that I might know the place for the first time.

I have remembered. And the remembering has revealed afternoons, days, and evenings without which I cannot conceive my life. Many of these jumped out of the reservoir unbidden, often with a fury that was astonishing, especially those I had held back for so long. But all of them, those repressed and those welcomed, are the weave of memory, which is in the end the continuity of any life—its story.

To be sure, it is artifice; we update and revise within the vagaries of time and age. But the act of writing, of organizing the weave within the black and white of the written word, somehow informs the process. I shall therefore remember it all now and in the future through the lens of this book, the truth of any of its instances by turns sharpened or blurred as this writing also folds itself into my past.

The writing of any history struggles against all our illusions. In the wider sense, the compendium of individual stories can provide the portrait of an age, and each may contribute something to our understanding of a particular period. But the final features of that portrait are drawn from those individual stories that remain after time and distance have sifted them all for relevance. And so, within that awareness, I place mine alongside some of the others, hoping some clarity may emerge from the mix. At the very least, by returning to the road to Lame Deer as it is traced in this writing, I can at last understand the persistence of certain memories:

The relentless walk of two children
who search through the dust of an Ashland afternoon
for lost parents

Four spheres of moist earth on a dinner plate
served in the absence of flute song

Arthritic fingers bent gently around
Polaroid pictures of a man in a coffin

A Thunderbird of coals
and the breath of the earth rising
from sandstone

The mirage of a man waist deep
in a beaver pond and his own joy

The smell of cedar, cottonwood, and sage
the faces of elders in firelight

A pack of children who plead for the noise of parody:
"Sing for us again!"
"Sing for us again!"

Again and again . . .

Postscript—2001

It is a warm mid-August afternoon, and Dick Littlebear and I are taking a ride up Muddy Creek Road. This had always been a favorite little road trip back then, when Tom, Dick, Henry, and I were (as Dick says now) the "Four Amigos." And as Dick's truck finds the ruts in the red clay road, we find our friendship—as we had left it thirty years ago—vital, full of humor and honesty.

Muddy Creek Road traverses one of the most beautiful areas on the reservation, and as we drive through it and our memories, it seems more luminous than ever. Our talk weaves through our personal histories, covering twenty-five years randomly, trying to say it all at once. Dick marks his recovery from alcoholism and his completion of a Ph.D. in Education as the turning points in his life. He loves his job as president of Dull Knife Memorial College in Lame Deer, which is celebrating ten years as a fully accredited junior college. And he is proud to be concurrently celebrating his own twenty years of sobriety. He's glad to know that I too am clean and sober.

"You know," he says, "I gave a commencement address last year at the high school. I told them, 'What you see in front of you is the town drunk who sobered up and became a college president.' They need to know they have choice. They don't have to go that other way. We have to stop hiding our problems."

We haven't had enough time over the past two days to catch up completely. Nonetheless, we have managed to lay the groundwork for an educational trust to be funded in part with proceeds from sales of this book and the photographs. The fund will be devoted to programs that support preservation of the Cheyenne language. Dick writes and speaks Cheyenne fluently, and this is a cause close to his heart. As he says, "When the language dies, the culture dies.

The youngest native speakers we have now are about forty years old. We need to bring the young ones along."

The road arches around pine-studded hills and climbs a little as our talk slowly finds its way to the reason for our journey up Muddy Creek. We are going to visit Henry Tall Bull's grave.

Dick scans the hillsides, looking for the little canyon that holds the Tall Bull family cemetery. Our conversation falters and disintegrates into silence. We've missed the turnoff. Dick makes a U-turn and we drive back in slow searching silence. "There it is," he says at last and makes the turn.

My return to Lame Deer has been nostalgic and wrenching and revelatory, with prodigal emotions always close to the surface. But now, as the truck comes to rest on this broad level spot tucked inside the belly of the plains, I am caught by the uncertainties of coincidence and synchronicity.

The hills around the little plateau are charred. Denuded burnt-black trees spike the horizon. Two years ago a massive forest fire cut through the reservation and left its mark here, sparing nothing but the graves. As we step out of the truck, one errant thunderhead, cut off from some distant storm, invades the clear sky and blots out the sun. The little plateau is hushed under cloud shade and sunburst. The cloud clings to the sun and bathes us in shadow as we approach the weathered fence surrounding the family plot. Dick steps between the wide boards to search for Henry's grave. I hesitate and feel the grief rise and stick in my throat. There is no visible headstone.

"Here it is," Dick says, "it's all caved in."

He looks at me, his eyes filled with a sadness I've never seen in him. I step through the fence and move close to him. He's holding a small, rectangular metal plate on which Henry's name and dates are embossed; and it's quite rusty around the edges.

"I guess nobody's been taking care of the graves. He should have more than just this tin marker."

I nod. My hand trembles as I touch his name. The cloud follows the sun and holds it tight. The shadow seems to crowd in, and then one gust of wind breaks the stillness and brushes my cheek.

My throat opens as I survey the grave. Sagebrush hugs the edges where the earth has dropped six inches or more into the rectangle. Near the spot where the steel marker had been, someone had placed a filter cigarette tobacco offering.

"What would it take to make this better?" I ask.

"Not much," he says. "We could fill it in, maybe get a stone."

And now we are very still within the half-light of the canyon. The sun draws bright lines around the perimeter of the thunderhead.

I pass through the fence again and move toward the truck. Dick is behind me. Suddenly, I pause and point to the backlit cloud. The words come before I can believe I'm saying them.

"The spirits are here with us today."

He regards me as one who has noted the obvious.

"Yes they are."

We drive away and let the road take us up to a higher plateau. And there, as if to echo all we have just experienced, a red-tailed hawk rises from behind a knoll and hovers, wings splayed against the updraft. He floats parallel to the truck for a while, then soars away.

Back in Lame Deer, we park at the college. I promise to return in the spring with a set of prints for the library. We say goodbye, shake hands, then quickly hug—tight—and quickly let go. As I turn and walk toward my car, he says, "Maybe when you come back in the spring we can fix Henry's grave."

Of course we will. I will return in the spring. There is no doubt. Some stories do not end.

PART II
A Tongue River Gallery

Illustrations

1. Henry Tall Bull

2. Lockwood Standing Elk

3. Willis Medicine Bull

4. Annie Medicine Bull

5. Albert Tall Bull

6. William Hollowbreast

7. Alex Black Horse

8–10. Grover Wolf Voice

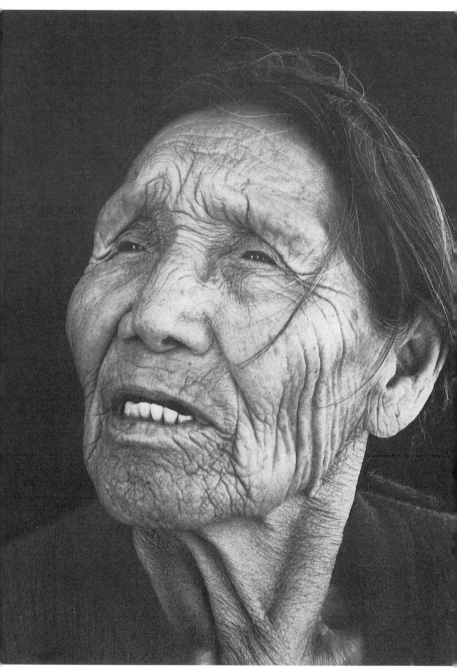

11. Bessie Elkshoulder

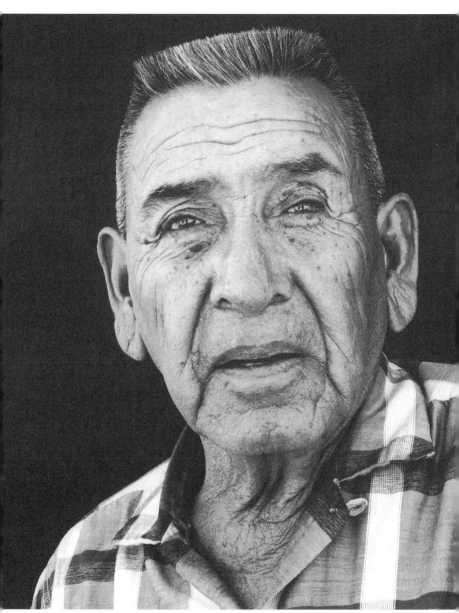

12. Ernest King (Ernest Mexican Cheyenne)

13. Belle Highwalking

14. George Highwalker

15. Hestahae (Donald Hollowbreast)

16. Josie Limpy

17. Mary Teeth

18. Erlyce Teeth

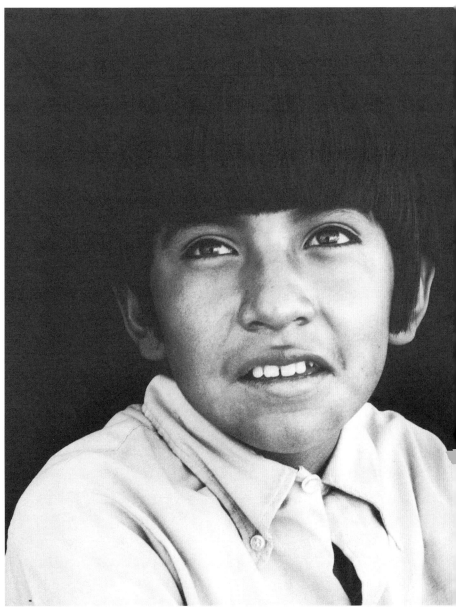

19. Terry Fisher

20. Henry Tall Bull butchering deer

21–24. Belle Highwalking
doing beadwork

25–31. George Highwalker performing rope tricks

32. Myrna at Belle's Cabin

33. Tom Weist

34. Sand-rock Island, Kirby Decker Road

35. Rosebud Creek

36. "Henry's Woman"

37. Iron Teeth (sitting), 1926. Buffalo Bill Historical Center,
Cody WY: Thomas Marquis Collection, P.165.1.77

38. Iron Teeth (standing), 1926. Buffalo Bill Historical Center,
Cody WY: Thomas Marquis Collection, P.165.1.80

39. Four Cheyenne Elders, 1922: (from left) Laban Little Wolf, Hairy Hand, Porcupine, Big Beaver. Buffalo Bill Historical Center, Cody WY: Thomas Marquis Collection, P.165.1.20

40. Black Bird, Keeper of the Sacred Buffalo Hat, 1928. Buffalo
Bill Historical Center, Cody wy: Thomas Marquis Collection,
p.165.1.39

41. Iron Shirt. Buffalo Bill Historical Center, Cody WY: Thomas Marquis Collection, P.165.1.31

42. Porcupine and His Wife, Wallowing Buffalo Woman. Buffalo
Bill Historical Center, Cody WY: Thomas Marquis Collection,
P.165.1.63

43. Busby Boarding School Girls. Buffalo Bill Historical Center, Cody WY: Thomas Marquis Collection, P.165.2.128

44. Lame Deer Baseball Team: (front row, from left) Frank Russel, William Hollowbreast, Lawrence Flying, Charles Spotted Wolf, (center row) Oliver Swallow, Fred Last Bull, John Woodenlegs, Fred Roundstone, (back row) Sam Weasel Bear, Henry Fisher, Tom Horse Roads, Hinton Leg. Buffalo Bill Historical Center, Cody WY: Thomas Marquis Collection, P.165.1.129

Appendix
Catalogue of Names and Dates

Through the devoted genealogical work of Timothy Cook in Busby, Montana, the following catalogue of names and dates was assembled. Each person is listed with his or her reservation name followed by maiden name in parentheses (where appropriate) and then their Cheyenne name (when known) and dates. All those listed here are deceased, though in several instances the date of death is unknown. For more information on Cheyenne genealogy, consult Timothy Cook's website: *www.cheyenneancestors.com*

Henry Tall Bull, Standing Twenty, 1917–1973

Belle Highwalking (Belle Teeth), ca. 1892–1971

Alex Black Horse, October 1897–?

Bessie Elkshoulder (Bessie Wandering Medicine),
    August 1893–?

Lockwood Standing Elk, Bird Nest, October 1889–?

Albert Tall Bull, April 1906–ca. 1972

William Hollowbreast, May 1900–?

Ernest King, also Ernest Mexican Cheyenne, December,
    1889–ca. 1978

Willis Medicine Bull, July 1887–?

Mary Teeth (Mary Long Roach), 15 April 1917–1993

Erlyce Teeth, 2 July 1956–12 January 2001

Josephine (Josie) Limpy (Josephine Headswift),
    Stands Near the Fire, June 1902–?

George Highwalker Sr., March 1913–ca. 1973

Donald Hollowbreast, Hestahae, 17 May 1917–26 June 2001

Annie Medicine Bull (Anna Swallow), May 1902–?

Grover C. Wolf Voice, April 1890–1978

Terry Fisher, no information available

Notes

To preserve the narrative flow of this text, which is a weave of personal experiences and some historical reference, I have omitted footnotes. Information and references uncommon enough to deserve citation are placed here by chapter and topic.

Preface

xii   I quote Paul Bowles from his book *The Sheltering Sky* (New York: Ecco Press, HarperCollins, 1999), 238.

Chapter One

4   The traditional Cheyenne response to death and dying described here is drawn largely from Thomas B. Marquis, *The Cheyennes of Montana*, ed. Thomas D. Weist (Algonac MI: Reference Publications, 1978), 221–31.

10   Accounts of the Custer fight are varied. These details are taken from James Welch with Paul Stekler, *Killing Custer* (New York: Penguin Books, 1995), 168–80; and Marquis, *The Cheyennes of Montana*, 242–63.

11   Throughout this book, "Agency" refers variously to "Indian Agency" (the Bureau of Indian Affairs) and the actual physical location of the BIA's official buildings on the reservation: i.e., "the Agency."

16   "Claims money" here refers to the settlement awarded to the Northern Cheyennes by the federal government through the Indian Court of Claims: $4,200,000 as redress for violations of the 1851 and 1868 Fort Laramie treaties. In addition to a per capita payment of $100 for each enrolled member, another $1,000 was allocated through a family plan which, in collaboration with the Tribal Council and the BIA, directed the use of funds. Many families used their funds to build new homes, renovate older ones, purchase mobile homes, or buy cattle.

Chapter Two

23   The kinship structures referred to are from Marquis, *The Cheyennes of Montana*, 174–84; and from John H. Moore, *The Cheyenne* (Cambridge MA: Blackwell, 1996), 152–58.

23–24 The discussion of Spirit People is drawn from Marquis, *The Cheyennes of Montana*, 146–56.

26   The account of suicide warriors (or suicide boys) derives from the personal battle narrative told by John Greany, a Southern Cheyenne, as it is recorded in Moore, *The Cheyenne*, 104–8.

29   "Honeyocker" is a somewhat derogatory name given to dry-land farmers who tried homesteading on the northern plains under the Kincaid Act in the 1920s. They tended to fail at the enterprise, usually after one or two growing seasons.

35   Weston La Barre's book on the Native American Church is *The Peyote Cult* (New York: Schocken Books, 1969).

Chapter Three

48   For the "Dead Indian Act," see Moore, *The Cheyenne*, 283–84.

Chapter Five

83–84 The account of the Cheyenne cattle business in the first decades of the twentieth century is from Tom Weist, *A History of the Cheyenne People* (Billings: Montana Council for Indian Education, 1977), 172–88; and Moore, *The Cheyenne*, 282–83.

86   The history of the Tongue River Irrigation Project (Birney Ditch) is recounted in Weist, *A History of the Cheyenne People*, 163–64.

87–88 The explanation of the Sacred Tipi is from Marquis, *The Cheyennes of Montana*, 137–45.

Chapter Six

115   Following the appearance of Hyemeyohsts Storm, *Seven Arrows* (New York: Harper & Row, 1972), Northern and Southern Cheyenne chiefs registered a formal protest with the publisher in 1975 claiming that the book grossly misrepresented Cheyenne ceremonies. They also refuted Storm's claim that he had been trained by Cheyenne elders. Harper & Row responded with a retraction that was included in subsequent editions of the book, the deletion of several sections of the text, and a small cash settlement paid to both branches of the tribe.

Chapter Seven

139   The references to the Battle of the Rosebud are from Welch and Stekler, *Killing Custer*, 120–24; and from Weist, *A History of the Cheyenne People*, 74–75.

Chapter Eight

144   The story of the death of Head Chief is from Weist, *A History of the Cheyenne People*, 136–37.